LEADING
MISSIONAL COMMUNITIES

Rediscovering the power of living on mission together

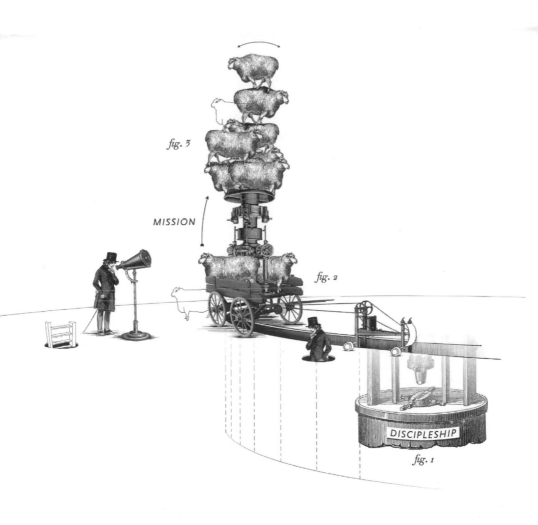

fig. 3

MISSION

fig. 2

DISCIPLESHIP

fig. 1

Mike Breen and the 3DM Team

First printing 2013
Printed in the United States of America
1 2 3 4 5 6 7 8 9 10 Printing/Year 16 15 14 13 12 11

Cover Design: Blake Berg
Interior Design: Pete Berg

ISBN: 978-0-9846643-8-2

CREDITS

Author	**Mike Breen**
Writers	**Ben Sternke**
	Rich Robinson
	Doug Paul
Editors	**Robert Neely**
	Eric Pfeiffer
Design	**Blake Berg**
	Pete Berg
Production	**Libby Culmer**

Support

Beccy Beresic	**Kimberly Berg**
Julie Bird	**Sally Breen**
Sam Breen	**Taylor Breen**
Craig Cheney	**Judy Cheney**
Gavin Culmer	**Angela Davila**
Anthony Davila	**Si Ford**
Joan Gooley	**Jessie Harrelson**
Kandi Pfeiffer	**Jo Rapps**
Kevin Rapps	**Courtney Reichley**
David Reichley	**Dave Rhodes**
Kim Rhodes	**Brandon Schaefer**
T.J. Schaefer	**Deb Sternke**
Patty Wyngaard	**Peter Wyngaard**

✄ TABLE OF CONTENTS ✄

A Brief Note About This Book Before Reading. i

Foreword v

Preface vii

PART 1: FOUNDATIONS for MCs

    Chapter 1:
    Understanding MCs and *Oikos* 3

    Chapter 2:
    Communities of Discipleship 13

    Chapter 3:
    Communities of Good News 21

    Chapter 4:
    Finding the Person of Peace 31

    Chapter 5:
    Both Organized and Organic 35

PART 2: LEADING MCs

    Chapter 6:
    Vision and Prayer 43

Chapter 7:

Three Examples **49**

Chapter 8:

Growing and Multiplying. **61**

PART 3: PRACTICAL TIPS

Chapter 9:

Why MCs Fail **79**

Chapter 10:

FAQ of MCs **89**

CONCLUSION:

Small Things With Great Love **107**

APPENDICES: NOTES FOR CHURCH LEADERS

Appendix 1:

It really is all about the discipling culture **113**

Appendix 2:

You go first: starting a pilot MC **117**

Appendix 3:

What about our current programs? **125**

Appendix 4:

MCs and church planting **133**

A BRIEF NOTE
∾ ABOUT THIS BOOK ∾
BEFORE READING

Although this is a stand-alone book, it falls within a trajectory of content that we have crafted for the teams of people who engage in our two-year Learning Community process. This particular book serves as the fourth and final book of this series.

Our core books, following the trajectory of the Learning Communities, each build on the content established in the previous books. They are the following:

- Building a Discipling Culture
- Multiplying Missional Leaders
- Leading Missional Communities
- Leading Kingdom Movements

Because of this approach, what appears to be "insider language" may show up from time to time as we reference points made in the previous books. However, we believe we've made a concerted effort to explain these points so this book can stand on its own. But to aid your understanding further, we wanted to share a few foundational terms we'll be using throughout the book.

Missional Leader
Someone who *mobilizes* God's people to join his redemptive work in the world.

Huddle
A discipleship vehicle for *leaders* that provides support, challenge, training, and accountability, and that is led by a discipling leader. Members eventually start Huddles of their own, creating a discipleship movement through multiplication.

Missional Frontier
Places or networks of people where there is little gospel presence and an opportunity for a much fuller in-breaking of the Kingdom of God.

Missional Community
A group of 20–50 people forming an extended family on mission together.

Oikos
The Greek word for "household," which refers to the 20–70 people, blood and non-blood, who made up the Greco-Roman household .

Character
Being like Jesus (the interior world of a person).

Competency
Doing the things Jesus could do (the external world of a person).

Disciple
- A person who learns to be like Jesus and learns to do what Jesus could do.
- Discipleship is the process of becoming who Jesus would be if he were you (Dallas Willard).
- Someone whose life and ministry reflect the life and ministry of Jesus.

UP/IN/OUT
As we see in the Gospels, Jesus had three great loves and thus three distinct dimensions to his life:
- UP: deep and connected relationship to his Father and attentiveness to the leading of the Holy Spirit.
- IN: constant investment in the relationships with those around him (disciples).

- OUT: entering into the brokenness of the world, looking for a response individually (people coming into a relationship with Jesus and his Father) and systemically (systems of injustice being transformed).

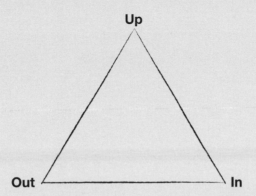

This three-dimensional pattern for living a balanced life is evident throughout scripture and needs to be expressed individually and in community life.

Kingdom Movements
A community that functions as a portal to the new world that God wants for all his children. A Kingdom movement is a community of disciples who passionately seek the expansion of God's reign here on earth through the reproduction of disciples, seeking the transformation of whatever places they inhabit.

Missional Sending Centers
Communities that have enough spiritual mass, with leaders who embody the character and competency of Jesus, to become places of reproducing, training and sending leaders into the missional frontier, as well as safe harbors of return and refreshment for these leaders whenever they leave a missional frontier, either temporarily or permanently.

✑ FOREWORD ✑

After 20 years of normal Sunday-based church experience, I moved to a new town with a handful of friends to start an intentional community of missionaries. We were partially motivated by our love of lost people, and equally motivated by a desire to experience more of God. We wanted to wake up every morning with the expectation that God had plans for us and that those plans would change the course of history for our friends.

It happened! Homes filled up, friends found faith in Jesus, and we began to see and feel the presence of God changing us to the core. Adullam is now a congregational network of missional communities and the several hundred people who belong to it would say, "We can't go back."

But, we also failed a lot. Whereas the size of our movement is credible, it's not nearly what it could have been if we had had a little help along the way; a little coaching, or a mentor-guide who had previously traversed the landscape we were trailblazing.

When I read this book, my first thought was, "Shucks, this could have saved us a lot of misery." Mike Breen and the entire 3DM team have emerged as expert coaches and practitioners to anyone who is sniffing the flower of missional community, true spiritual formation, and kingdom practices. This short, simple book is an overflow of their experience and practical wisdom, and should be a plumb line for every leader and every church that wants to make disciples of Jesus.

Regardless of your context or church paradigm, this book is foundational and will help you set new rails, new rhythms, and new practices that God will bless.

— Hugh Halter, author of *The Tangible Kingdom* and
AND: the Gathered and Scattered Church.

∾ PREFACE ∾

Our previous book on Missional Communities (MCs), *Launching Missional Communities*, was a helpful tool for guiding church leaders toward understanding and pioneering MCs.

However, as we coached and consulted with pastors and church leaders over the past several years in our Learning Communities, we discovered something. It's one thing to learn how to *launch* MCs, but another thing entirely to learn how to *lead* them well so they become a reproducing hotbed for discipleship and mission in churches.

For this reason, we decided to go back to the drawing board and write a book that focused on the processes and principles of leading an MC so that it can multiply in a healthy way. Our overarching goal is to put discipleship and mission back into the hands of ordinary people. So, this book is written with the ordinary person in mind. We hope that everyone can use this book to learn the basic principles of launching, leading, and multiplying MCs. We hope you enjoy reading it and trying it out!

PART 1

∽ FOUNDATIONS FOR ∽
MCs

1
∾ UNDERSTANDING ∾ MCs AND *OIKOS*

A FEAST FOR EVERYONE

It's almost noon, and the house is saturated with the rich scent of roasted turkey, sweet potatoes, and pumpkin pie. Every family or friend invited prepared and brought food to share with everyone else. A few people came over early to help Mom and Dad make sure the house was ready for guests.

Some of the adults and older children are finishing up a game of touch football in the backyard while a few of the younger kids play tag. Your uncle brought a friend from work, a die-hard Detroit Lions fan who is glued to the TV with a couple of other people taking in the pregame show. Several others are talking in the kitchen as they put the finishing touches on the Thanksgiving feast they will all be eating in 20 minutes or so.

After sitting down at the table with one another for a laid-back, longer-than-usual lunch filled with laughter and connection, the day will continue—together. Some will begin putting away leftovers and washing the dishes. Some will immediately settle into chairs and couches for the football game (and probably a nap). Some will go back outside to play more touch football. Some will strike up conversations with cousins they haven't seen in a while.

Eventually, those who are hungry will get the leftovers back out for an informal supper. Some will be reading a beloved book on the couch, while others will be talking. The gathering will last well into the evening. Some will need to go home; others will spend the night. Before adjourning, they'll make plans to do things tomorrow.

This portrait of an extended family celebrating Thanksgiving is a distinctly American story, of course, but the same basic plot exists across the globe. The language, food, and geography may be different, but the theme is the same.

EXTENDED FAMILIES ON MISSION

It may sound strange to start talking about Missional Communities by talking about an extended family gathering around the Thanksgiving table. But that's where we have to begin. Why? Because, ultimately, **we don't want to talk about Missional Communities. We want to talk about family.**
Bear with us as we explain ourselves a bit.

MCs ARE NOT
a silver bullet
that will solve all
of the church's
missional
problems.

FAMILY

Missional Communities (MCs) are a hot topic right now in the church, and many are excited about the potential of MCs to help the church live out its mission in the world. We began using MCs in the 1990s and are now helping to lead the church in implementing them. (That's probably why you're reading this book.) However, **MCs are not a silver bullet** that will solve all of the church's missional problems. Although MCs are not the destination, they are enormously valuable, because MCs are a structure that helps us get to our true goal, **something we call *oikos*.**

Oikos is a Greek word used in the New Testament to refer to "households," which were essentially extended families who functioned together with a common purpose. In the early church, discipleship and mission always centered around and flourished in the *oikos*. This vehicle facilitated the relational dynamic that allowed the church to thrive in the midst of persecution and hardship for hundreds of years. *Oikos* still helps the church thrive today, even in places where persecution is quite severe. We are absolutely convinced that *oikos* is what the church needs to reclaim if it is going to become the kind of movement the church was in its earliest days.

SEEMS A LOT FOR MC TO REPLACE

In fact, living as *oikos* has been the norm for almost every culture for most of human history. It's just how family was—not 2.4 children in a single-family home but a wider community sharing life and work and celebration and

FAMILY

commerce together. Only in the last hundred years or so in the West have we lost this sense of being extended families on mission. For a whole host of reasons, we have unwittingly embraced the fragmentation of the extended family and tried to live primarily as individuals and nuclear families. The results of this experiment have been utterly disastrous, and you probably see the aftermath all around you. Loneliness and depression are rampant, we are more stressed and busier than ever, and many people feel they are barely keeping their heads above water as they try to advance in their careers, raise their children, and seek some semblance of meaning in life.

In the midst of this sea of chaos and confusion, however, those of us who follow Christ have the remarkable opportunity to literally rebuild society by re-forming "extended family" *oikos* communities centered not on blood or ancestry, but on Jesus. Our commission is to compassionately reach out to those around us, invite them to join us in community, share the story of the gospel, make disciples, and gather them into families to follow Jesus together. That's really what starting an MC is all about. This is not a fad or the latest church growth technique or a new name for cell groups. It is rediscovering the church as *oikos*, an extended family on mission where everyone contributes and everyone is supported.

STARTING AN MC is about rediscovering the church as *oikos*, an extended family on mission where everyone contributes and everyone is supported.

So, it isn't that MCs aren't important. They are, and that's why we wrote this book. But MCs are simply the initial vehicle we learn to drive that gets us to the real destination: learning to live as *oikos*, extended families functioning together on mission with God. MCs are the training wheels that teach us how to ride the bike of *oikos*. They are the scaffolding that allows us to rebuild the household of *oikos*. MCs are the cocoon that allows the butterfly of *oikos* to emerge. You get the picture. In fact, we think that in 50 years, people will look back and say, "It's hilarious—they used to make people join MCs because they didn't know how to do this! Isn't that amazing?"

We believe *oikos* is something the Spirit of God is doing in this time to restore the church's ability to function fruitfully in discipleship and mission the way the early church did, publicly living out our faith in the various neighborhoods and relational networks of our cities. We firmly believe this is *the* make-or-break issue for the Western church. We simply will not see God's dream for the world come true unless we learn how to function as extended families on mission.

The good news is that it isn't actually that complicated, and God will give us the power to do it. This isn't a task reserved for church leaders, pastors, or experts—it's for everyone! When MCs are led well, they are an extremely effective vehicle for training ordinary people to follow Jesus together and re-learn *oikos*, so we want to equip you as practically as possible to do this. But remember: The goal is not to run a program called "Missional Community." The goal is to learn how to function as an extended family on mission. We really believe this is something *everyone* can learn to do.

Think of it like this: MCs are a great vehicle with a powerful engine (discipleship, but we'll get to that in a bit), but the thing about a vehicle is that it's supposed to take you somewhere. The destination the vehicle of MC takes us to is *oikos*. To drive successfully and purposefully, you need to know where you're going, and you need to know how to drive the vehicle. That's what you'll find in this book.

A quote widely attributed to Margaret Mead captures the idea well: "Never doubt that a small group of thoughtful, committed [people] can change the world. Indeed it's the only thing that ever has."[1]

Consider this your invitation to join a movement to change the world by simply building an extended family on mission.

WHAT IS A MISSIONAL COMMUNITY?

Before we dive into the principles and practicalities of starting and leading MCs, we need to start by defining what an MC is and describe some of the features that distinguish it from other kinds of vehicles the church has used. "Missional Community" has become a bit of a buzzword in the church, and people have used the term in a variety of ways. However, when we talk about MCs, we are talking about something quite specific. Here's our definition:

....

[1] Attributed to Margaret Mead in Frank G. Sommers and Tana Dineen (1984), *Curing Nuclear Madness,* p. 158

adults - our goal - 15 adults

A Missional Community is a group of approximately **20 to 40 people** who are seeking to **reach a particular neighborhood or network of relationships with the good news of Jesus**. The group functions as a flexible, local expression of the church and has the expressed intention of seeing those they are in relationship with become followers of Jesus with them. They exist to see God's Kingdom come to their friends and neighbors. The result is usually the growth of the MC (as people become followers of Jesus and join them) and then the multiplication of new MCs (as people are trained to lead within the MC and then are sent out to start new MCs). They are networked within a larger church community, allowing for a "scattered" and "gathered" expression of church.

These **lightweight, low-maintenance**, mid-sized communities, **led by lay people**, typically have three to four "official" meetings per month in their missional context. (This means that *when* they meet, *where* they meet, *with whom* they meet, and *what they do* when they meet are highly contextualized, determined by the vision and missional context of the MC.) Because they hold a strong value of "doing life" together, the people in the MC often meet with one another outside the "official" gatherings in more informal settings during the week. In structured and spontaneous ways, each MC **attends to the three dimensions of life** that Jesus himself attended to: time with God through worship, prayer, Scripture, teaching, giving thanks, etc. (what we call UP); time with the body of believers, building a vibrant and caring community (what we call IN); and time with those who don't know Jesus yet (what we call OUT).

Let's break this down into **five characteristics** that will make MCs easy to define.

1) 20 — 40 PEOPLE

This is an approximate figure rather than a hard rule, because MCs vary in size depending on culture and context. We'll talk more about this later in the book, but for now, note that size *does* matter in MCs. They must be *mid-sized* communities, bigger than small groups but smaller than whole churches,

MCs MUST BE
small enough
to care, but
big enough to
dare.

because they must be **small enough to care but also big enough to dare**. What do we mean by this?

MCs are **small enough to care** because a group of 20–40 feels like an extended family where everyone can be known and loved and contribute meaningfully to the community. Because an MC is generally smaller than a whole church, it is much easier for individuals to find a place of belonging and feel like they are a vital part of a community. The small size also creates a more comfortable environment for a new person coming into the community, because 20–40 people create a "house party" dynamic that provides a semi-anonymous space in the community for people to hang out on the margins and observe before they move in closer for more in-depth participation. Small groups of six to 12 people don't have this kind of space, and visiting a group of this size is often quite intimidating for a new person.

MCs are **big enough to dare** because a group of 20–40 people has enough human resource to substantively impact their chosen mission context, whether it's a neighborhood or a network of relationships. In other words, they can get more done because there are more people involved than in a small group! In addition, multiplication is much easier with a group of 20–40 people. One of the reasons small groups don't tend to multiply is that people don't want to part with the close friends they've cultivated in the small group. Multiplying an MC, however, allows you to continue the journey with your closest friends while still expanding the Kingdom of God by fulfilling the Great Commission.

2) CLEAR MISSION VISION

my original thought for an MC

It is vital that an MC gathers around a vision for mission *from the beginning*. If you don't have a well-defined missional vision at the start of an MC's life, it is difficult to bring a vision in later, because the group almost always becomes a social club for Christians or a Bible study. Missional vision means you have a desire and passion to share the good news of Jesus with a specific group of people through your words and your actions. Clearly seeing and articulating this vision is the **magnet** that draws people to the community and the **engine** that keeps the community moving.

Missional vision is focused on *sharing the good news of Jesus* and *making disciples* among the people of a specific **neighborhood** or **network of**

relationships. A neighborhood-focused MC centers on serving and bringing the good news of Jesus to the people who live or work in a particular geographic area (e.g., a housing subdivision or a few blocks of streets). A network-focused MC seeks to serve and bring the good news of Jesus to the people within a particular network of relationships (e.g., a sports club, creative professionals, a hobby group, a business community, students, a subculture in the city, etc.). Giving your MC a specific name, perhaps related to its vision, often helps to keep the vision forefront in people's minds, and establishes a sense of identity and belonging within the MC.

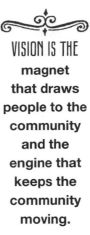

VISION IS THE **magnet that draws people to the community and the engine that keeps the community moving.**

As we think about bringing the good news to people in a neighborhood or relational network, remember that an MC doesn't just swoop in and do a few activities for a group and then leave. The MC emphasizes living among and working with the people or place they are seeking to impact. This "incarnational principle" helps prevent MCs from becoming a series of service projects performed by people who are disconnected relationally from those they are serving.

> *"The most vigorous forms of community are those that come together in the context of a shared ordeal or communities who define themselves as a group with a mission that lies beyond themselves — thus initiating a risky journey. Over-concern with safety and security, combined with comfort and convenience, have lulled us out of our true calling and purpose."*
> — Alan Hirsch and Michael Frost, *The Forgotten Ways*

3) LIGHTWEIGHT / LOW-MAINTANENCE

Every effort should be put into making MCs as lightweight and low maintenance as possible. This means they are inexpensive to run, not too time-consuming to plan, and not bound by building or maintenance costs. Leading an MC shouldn't be a heavy burden on a leader. People with normal "9–5 jobs" should be able to lead them. For example, MC gatherings shouldn't attempt to replicate a church worship service, because those take a lot of time and hard work to plan and maintain! Instead, look to implement regular, sustainable rhythms that allow people to connect as family. (More on this later, but what we're talking about is "recycling" time by missionally focusing the activities we are already involved in, rather than adding more events and extra commitments to the calendar.) Build a team around you to help lead and organize the various aspects of the community, releasing the body of Christ to function well together.

IT'S ABOUT learning to live a missional lifestyle together, not attending a series of missional events.

Remember this is about building an extended family on mission together, so let the idea of "family rhythms" guide your thinking. Have everyone bring food to share for meals together. Maybe have some people come over early to help clean up the house before the others arrive. Have everyone stick around afterward to do the dishes and help clean up—like a family would! **It's about learning to live a missional lifestyle together, not attending a series of missional events.**

4) AN ACCOUNTABLE LEADER

MCs are led by leaders with vision, but those leaders are **accountable to and supported by the leadership of the wider church**. MCs are not church plants (at least not in the traditional sense). They continue to be part of a larger whole, orbiting a central church, where they receive training and support. This creates a **low-control, high-accountability** dynamic that is vital to MC health. **Low control** means that the vision for the MC comes from the leader of the MC, not the central church leadership. **High accountability** means that the central church leadership is very involved in helping the MC leader carry out the vision God has given him or her. The MCs become places of on-the-ground mission for the people of God, dispersed among the neighborhoods and networks of a city, but still orbiting a central church, which becomes a place of training, equipping, prayer, resourcing, and encouragement for the MCs.

Each MC has a regular orbit around the central church, depending on the MC's context and needs. Some communities come to Sunday gatherings most weeks and meet in their mission context mostly on weekdays. Other communities may meet in their mission context most weekends and come to a Sunday gathering just once a month—or anything in between! Again, this is determined by the vision and mission context of the MC, and is agreed on in a dialogue between the MC leader and the church leadership.

5) UP / IN / OUT RHYTHM

MCs center their rhythms on growing in relationship with God (UP), with one another (IN), and with those they are reaching out to (OUT). This is community life centered on the Great Commandment and the Great Commission:

- "Love the Lord your God with all your heart, mind soul and strength" (UP).
- "Love your neighbor as yourself" (IN).
- "Go and make disciples of all people groups" (OUT).

Again, remember that we are not talking about merely scheduling a series of events for people to attend. We are talking about communicating vision and establishing rhythms and routines that allow us to become an extended family on mission together. To do this, we need rhythms that connect us with God in worship and prayer (UP), with each other in deeper community (IN), and with those in our mission context in love and service (OUT).

These are the key characteristics that define successful MCs. Now let's move on to foundations upon which MCs are built.

2

∾ COMMUNITIES OF ∾ DISCIPLESHIP

So now that we have defined what an MC is, **what would it look like for you to start one?** Where would you start? What would you need to know? What are the practical tools you'll need to have the best chance of success?

As you think about setting off on this exciting journey, we want to lay out **four foundational principles** that we have found to be vital as we've seen hundreds of people launch and lead MCs. In our experience, these seem to be non-negotiable principles. Basically, MCs really don't work very well unless all four of these principles are in place and functioning well. In other words, this section is worth reading slowly, and perhaps coming back to again as you begin to make plans for launching your MC.

FOUNDATION 1: COMMUNITIES OF DISCIPLESHIP

A common misconception of MCs is that they are simply a way to get people out to do service projects in the community every once in a while. But MCs must be communities where real discipleship takes place, or they won't become places of *oikos* and will never multiply in a healthy way.

One MC leader recalls:

> "Our MC was reaching out to the homeless who gathered at a certain park on Saturday mornings. Originally, we were bringing sack lunches and survival kits. Part of the MC was getting these hand-outs together each week, and another part was going down on Saturday mornings to hand them out. However, our city actually has some wonderful social services for the homeless. You can

always get a bed, shower and food. What we noticed, though, was that they didn't have any friends; no one would actually talk to them. So we changed everything. We made it much more simple and relational. When we visited them on Saturday mornings, we'd wait for others who were there to give them hand-outs, and then we'd set up tables and play checkers and chess and have coffee. As we got to know them, we'd pray with them, ask for ways we could serve them, share what God had been saying to us, and ask them to share what God might have been sharing with them. It was amazing to see what God was able to do when we switched from seeing our MC as a series of event or service projects to a family where we were trying to create a certain kind of culture."

The first principle is that you'll need to build a **discipling culture** at the heart of your MC if it is going to be fruitful long-term. At the core of *every* effective MC is a culture of discipleship. Far more important than the infrastructure we put in place or the rhythms we establish is the culture we are growing in our MC through the rhythm and infrastructure. Culture trumps programs or events *every time.*

YOU'LL NEED to build a discipling culture at the heart of your MC if it is going to be fruitful long-term.

What do we mean by a **discipling culture**? A culture is kind of like what water is to a fish, or what soil and air are to a plant. It's the environment within which the whole thing exists. And just as certain kinds of soils make for better gardens than others, certain kinds of cultures make for better MCs than others. Just as you need the very best soil if you want a fruitful garden, you need a discipling culture if you want a successful and fruitful MC. Think of discipleship as the "ecosystem" of your MC. A discipling culture simply means that **making disciples of Jesus is what is always happening in your MC**.

The Great Commission is to make disciples. Jesus says that he will build his church,[2] and our task is to make disciples.[3] Sometimes we get this backward and think that if we can figure how to build the church, then the end result

....

[2] Matthew 16:18

[3] Matthew 28:19-20

will be disciples. But it actually works the other way around: We make disciples, and Jesus builds his church. Thus, the culture and mindset we want to build in our MCs is a **discipling culture**, where people understand clearly that we are called to both *be* and *make* disciples of Jesus.

This means that within an MC, we are learning to trust and follow Jesus in every area of our lives, growing to become more and more like him in our character (who we are) and competency (what we can do). As we do this, we invite others to share this life of discipleship with us, growing in expectation that God's Kingdom will break into every area of our lives. We cultivate an identity as a "sent" people, missionaries to whatever sphere of influence or context we find ourselves in. As we truly make disciples (people who are becoming the same kind of person as Jesus was and doing the things he did), evangelism becomes a kind of overflow of our life of discipleship, rather than a program or event. Instead of feeling forced or contrived, evangelism will feel natural as people are drawn in by the fruit they see in our community.

A discipling culture is about encouraging and cultivating the development of a missional *lifestyle* (faith at the center of everything we do) rather than missional *events* (faith at the center of events we organize).

So how do we make sure there is a culture of discipleship developing at the center of our MC? We start by looking at the way Jesus did it. Within the wider group of people who followed him, he gathered 12 people to be with him and learn from him in a more intentional way. They watched what he did, ate with him and one another, talked together, played together, prayed together, worked together. Eventually, Jesus sent them out to do some of the same things together they were watching him do,[4] and they began to actually do the things Jesus himself had been doing. They came back together, and Jesus coached them,[5] challenged them,[6] encouraged them,[7] and sent them

> ## MAKING
> disciples of Jesus is what is always happening in your MC.

---

[4] Luke 9:1-6

[5] Luke 9:10

[6] Luke 9:13

[7] Luke 9:28-36

out again. When they returned, he again debriefed, encouraged, coached, and rejoiced with them.[8]

In all of this, Jesus moved his disciples toward the goal of having the capacity to be the kind of person he is (character) and do the kinds of things he does (competency). His goal is that they would have the same kind of life within themselves that Jesus had within himself. "I tell you the truth," Jesus told them late in his ministry, "whoever believes in me will do the works I have been doing, and they will do even greater things than these, because I am going to the Father" (John 14:12). Jesus' goal was that they would be able to the same kinds of things as he was doing, because they were becoming the same kind of people.

We also see this dynamic in the life of the apostle Paul. As he traveled around planting churches (communities that probably looked a lot like MCs), he always had a team with him, people he was training to do the same things he was doing. In a letter to the church communities of Corinth, he writes,

> "I am writing this not to shame you but to warn you as my dear children. Even if you had ten thousand guardians in Christ, you do not have many fathers, for in Christ Jesus I became your father through the gospel. Therefore I urge you to imitate me. For this reason I have sent to you Timothy, my son whom I love, who is faithful in the Lord. He will remind you of my way of life in Christ Jesus" (1 Cor 4:14-16).

He wanted the Corinthian believers to *imitate him* as children imitate their father or mother. Since he couldn't come to Corinth himself to be their example, *he sent Timothy*, because Timothy would remind them of Paul's way of life. In other words, Paul was saying, "I can't come to you right now, but I'm sending someone who has become the same kind of person as me. Timothy will remind you of me just like a son reminds people of his father, because I have become his spiritual father, and he has become my spiritual son." Isn't that remarkable?

Paul urged Timothy to continue this reproducing pattern, because **every disciple of Jesus should eventually be capable of making more disciples of Jesus.** Part of *being* a disciple is *making* disciples. So Paul wrote to his disciple Timothy, "the things you have heard me say in the presence of

[8] Luke 10:1-24

many witnesses entrust to reliable people who will also be qualified to teach others."[9] **That's four generations of disciples in one sentence!** Paul (first generation) investing in Timothy (second generation), who invests in "reliable people" (third generation) who are to invest in "others" (fourth generation).

Discipleship, as Dallas Willard has noted, is simply being with Jesus to learn from Jesus how to be like Jesus.[10] We do this best in community, in relationship with people who are more like Jesus than we are—by learning from them, observing them, doing life with them, being involved in a highly challenging, highly encouraging relationship in which we learn how to do the things that Jesus did by imitating the "way of life in Christ" of someone else. Then we invite others to imitate us as we imitate Christ.[11]

Establishing a culture where this kind of process is normal and expected is the end goal of any MC, because we want to actually live out the kind of life we invite others into.

Even if it isn't fully present right away, creating a **discipling culture** needs to be something every MC is working toward from the very beginning. A strong discipling culture leads naturally to the development of an abundant supply of new leaders, who, because they are living like Jesus and listening to the Spirit, will make more disciples and plant new MCs that contain the same **culture of discipleship** you have established. The **discipling culture** and **missional leaders** you are developing function "below the surface" as the foundation of any effective and fruitful MC.

---

[9] 2 Timothy 2:2

[10] Ben Sternke, a member of our team, heard Willard give this definition during an informal conversation

[11] 1 Corinthians 11:1

Looking at the pattern of Jesus, then, what are some practical things we can do to keep a discipling culture at the heart of an MC?

COMMON LANGUAGE

Jesus created a common language among his disciples by telling parables of the Kingdom over and over again. These oft-repeated word pictures functioned as the language that allowed him to create a culture of discipleship among his followers.

This lines up perfectly with what sociologists have discovered: Language creates culture. So if we want a discipling culture to take root in our MCs, we need to be intentional about using a common **language of discipleship** that everyone understands and uses regularly. This language should be something that's very simple and easy to remember. Because people today are so visually oriented in their thinking, we recommend using the visual "language" of **LifeShapes** to create a culture of discipleship.[12]

You'll need to be intentional about this at first, because it won't feel natural to use the discipling language initially. But as you persist in repeatedly using the vocabulary and living it out practically, it inevitably creates a culture of discipleship.

"At first I was pretty resistant to implementing this discipling language and using shapes as a way of remember them and passing them on," one MC leader said. "I mean seriously, shapes? But I agreed to try them for a while, and I couldn't believe how helpful having a consistent discipling language was. It changed the culture of our MC faster than I could have imagined. People I had been unable to get to do anything were suddenly bringing ideas to the table and asking if they could run with them. It was incredible."

Recently, a middle-aged woman came to a church where this discipling language was being used. Initially, she found it off-putting and hard to engage with, calling it "jargon." But as she grew in relationship with one of the leaders, she joined a Huddle (a vehicle for intentionally discipling and training leaders) and found that, as she heard the language used in a relational context and

....

[12] You can learn more about LifeShapes in our book *Building a Discipling Culture.*

intentionally expressed in life (not just talked about abstractly), it became very helpful. Now she understands the need for and the value of a discipling language and has started using it herself, not just as information but as a lifestyle.

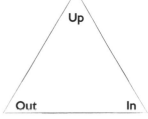

We have seen it happen again and again, in almost every conceivable cultural situation. It is remarkable, for example, how simply drawing a triangle and talking about an "UP/IN/OUT" life begins to create a culture where people have a sense of being sent "OUT," almost without even trying! Consistent training in and expression of a discipling language really do create a discipling culture.

COMMON RHYTHMS

In addition to a common discipling language, our MCs also need **common rhythms** that we regularly participate in, predictable patterns that instill a sense of stability in the community. The regular routines we engage in shape our lives deeply, affecting our mindset, outlook, and sense of identity and purpose. To grow a culture of discipleship, **we need to be together a lot**, participating in common rhythms of discipleship centered on deepening our relationship with God (UP), our relationship with one another (IN), and our relationship with our mission context (OUT). We can't develop a culture of discipleship unless we actually get together *often* as an extended family. We'll talk more about this in a bit.

DISCIPLING LEADER & HUDDLE

Finally, you simply don't get a discipling culture unless someone takes the responsibility to lead it. **The leader of an MC needs to be a disciple-maker, not merely an event-organizer.** Part of your responsibility as an MC leader is to look for and invest in potential leaders, considering things like godly character, skills, and whether the person already

THE LEADER
of an MC needs to be a disciple-maker, not merely an event-organizer.

influences others positively. You sow the seeds of multiplication by discipling and training these people as leaders. Invite potential leaders into a more intentional discipling relationship within the MC (giving them greater access to your life and training them in Huddle), and begin having them function on a leadership team within the MC, giving them growing responsibility and visibility as leaders in the MC.

This will sow the seeds of multiplication within your MC, because as these leaders grow in their character and competency, they will begin to have vision for what God wants to do through their life. New MCs can be birthed, because they'll have a new discipling leader with vision. Remember that the point of MCs isn't simply to create a space for people to experience community; we are called to participate in the advance of the Kingdom of God by making disciples who become leaders and multiply to make more disciples. This is why having a discipling culture at the heart of your MC is so important. We never truly multiply without it.

3

∾ COMMUNITIES OF ∾ GOOD NEWS

A second foundational element of launching an MC is thinking deeply about the gospel. We need to do this for several reasons. First, we need to make sure we understand all of what we want MCs to do, because they aren't just clever vehicles to bolster church membership or organize service projects in the community. This vehicle (and the family on mission an MC is meant to produce) **is all about the good news of Jesus**. MCs exist to draw people into new life in Christ. It's about making disciples of Jesus and seeing them transformed in community as they follow him. If we don't understand the nature of the gospel as it is fleshed out in community, we won't ever truly understand what we are unlocking with MCs, and their full potential will remain untapped.

> *"The Church exists for nothing else but to draw men into Christ, to make them little Christs. If they are not doing that, all the cathedrals, clergy, missions, sermons, even the Bible itself, are simply a waste of time. God became Man for no other purpose."*
> — C.S. Lewis

MORE THAN FORGIVENESS

Another reason we need to focus on the gospel is that many of us have inherited a truncated version of the gospel that doesn't tell the whole story of the good news of Jesus. If MCs are going to be "good news communities" and proclaim the gospel effectively, we need to have a fuller, more robust picture of what the gospel actually is. For example, if we proclaim a gospel that has to do only with forgiveness of sins, we typically don't end up with disciples of Jesus. Instead, we usually create what Dallas Willard called "vampire Christians"—people who are interested in Jesus only for his blood.[13] For people who think the gospel is only about having their sins forgiven so they can go to heaven someday, discipleship is an optional extra-curricular activity. Following Jesus now isn't terribly compelling because the "deal" they signed up for is simply a contract to go to heaven when they die. We need to recover a fuller, more biblical picture of the gospel. While it isn't something *less than* forgiveness (that's certainly part of it), it's a lot *more than* just forgiveness.

The gospel that Jesus and all the New Testament writers proclaimed was simply **the present availability of life in the Kingdom of God to everyone through trusting Jesus.**[14] It's the good news that you can begin a new kind of life with God right now by placing your trust in Jesus and his words. It's an invitation to participate now in the life of God, joining him in what he's doing right now on Earth. Life under God's rule is available to anyone who wants it, and we enter that life by trusting Jesus (which is what "believing in" him means). That's the good news Jesus and the apostles preached. Of course, it includes forgiveness of sins (thank God!), but also so much more than that.

COVENANT & KINGDOM

How does this understanding of the gospel play out, then? As you may know from other resources we've published, our foundational understanding of Scripture is rooted in the two over-arching themes of **Covenant** and **Kingdom**. Right at the beginning of Genesis and all the way through to Revelation, we are called into a **relationship** with God (Covenant) and the **responsibility** of representing him to others (Kingdom). In Genesis, Adam and Eve walk with God in the cool of the evening (Covenant), and are commissioned to multiply, thus filling and stewarding the earth (Kingdom). When we look at the life of Jesus, we see him build a discipling culture by bringing to those who followed him an **invitation to a Covenant relationship** and a **challenge to join God in the mission of the Kingdom**. As people engaged in this amazing relationship

---

[13] In his masterpiece *The Divine Conspiracy*, Willard calls the forgiveness-only gospel a "Gospel of Sin Management" and says such gospels "foster 'vampire Christians' who only want a little blood for the their sins but nothing more to do with Jesus until heaven" (p. 403, n. 8).

[14] Paul's way of understanding this was "citizenship" (Philippians 3:20).

with Jesus and the adventure of the Kingdom mission, the natural outcome was that the disciples became a dynamic **community on mission**, their adventures chronicled mainly in the book of Acts.[15]

Here's a diagram that may help us see how these things played out for Jesus and his disciples.

COVENANT	and	KINGDOM
RELATIONSHIP	and	RESPONSIBILITY
INVITATION	and	CHALLENGE
COMMUNITY	on	MISSION

Likewise, the fuller, more robust definition of the gospel we embrace also plays out along the lines of Covenant and Kingdom, as the gospel focuses on the good news of Christ's **substitution** on our behalf, how he took on the wrath we deserved (Covenant), and his **victory** over the powers of darkness, defeating the enemy who held us in bondage (Kingdom).

COVENANT	and	KINGDOM
RELATIONSHIP	and	RESPONSIBILITY
INVITATION	and	CHALLENGE
COMMUNITY	on	MISSION
SUBSTITUTION	and	VICTORY

To see how this plays out in Scripture, take a look at Paul's articulation of the gospel in Colossians 2:13-15 below. It seamlessly weaves in **substitution** and **victory**, like the threads of a tapestry, or two sides of the same coin:

> When you were dead in your sins and in the uncircumcision of your flesh, God made you alive with Christ. He forgave us all our sins, having canceled the charge of our legal indebtedness, which stood against us and condemned us; he has taken it away, nailing it to the cross. And having disarmed the powers and authorities, he made a public spectacle of them, triumphing over them by the cross.

....

[15] To understand more about how these themes play out in Scripture, pick up a copy of our book *Covenant and Kingdom: The DNA of the Bible* from our online store at www.weare3dm.com.

THE GOOD NEWS OF CHRIST'S VICTORY

Paul articulates **victory** when he says that Christ has "disarmed the powers and authorities" and "made a public spectacle of them, triumphing over them by the cross." Paul is invoking an image of what happened to convicted traitors who were about to be executed. The traitors were marched publicly through the city streets in chains so that everyone could see them before they were put to death. People would come out in throngs to see the public spectacle of the march, as well as the torture and eventual death of the prisoners. The public march indicated that their fate was sealed, even though they hadn't been executed yet.

Paul's readers would have remembered that Jesus was taken through the streets in this kind of public march as he carried his cross to his place of execution. It appeared initially that evil had triumphed. However, we discovered after the resurrection that Jesus had actually turned the tables on Satan and won the victory through the very act that looked like defeat. It was almost as if God had tricked Satan into over-playing his hand. The early church fathers said that our enemy, when he struck Jesus with his sword, was unable to take the sword out of Jesus' body. The instrument of evil that had enslaved all of humanity remained in Jesus, effectively disarming our enemy.

Suddenly, the public spectacle is reversed, and it's actually our enemy who has been disarmed and marched through the streets! Now, through the death and resurrection of Jesus, all the instruments of evil and injustice that have held humanity under their dominion have been defeated: death, sin, sadness, sickness, shame, disease, injustice, oppression. Jesus is the victor! He has triumphed over evil by the cross. He is our champion.

For the first thousand years or so of church history, this was the dominant understanding of what was accomplished on the cross. They called this theme *Christus Victor* (meaning "Christ is victorious!"). When people thought about the gospel, what came to mind first was God's victory over the forces of evil through the cross of Christ.

This means that one facet of the good news for people today is that **through the death and resurrection of Christ, God has won the victory over everything that holds them in bondage**. There is freedom in Christ! Because of the same Spirit that raised Christ from the dead lives in us, we represent Jesus, the victorious King. And as we implement God's victory over evil *now* in our own lives and communities, we are able to invite others into the same experience of freedom that we enjoy.

This is part of the gospel we proclaim to those we are seeking to reach in our MCs: Christ is victorious over evil! All of the healing, redemption, and victory that we will one day see in totality and completeness in heaven is *already* coming to earth right now. Today. The world begins to look different because the victory of his Kingdom is coming and his will is beginning to be done in our communities just as it is in heaven. The challenge to us as God's people is to make sure that our lives are manifesting the freedom we proclaim, making sure the message of our lives matches the message of our words.

THE GOOD NEWS OF CHRIST'S SUBSTITUTION

Paul articulates another facet of the gospel in this passage, that of **substitution**. He says that while we were dead in our sins, God forgave our sins and made us alive with Christ. "He forgave all our sins, having canceled the charge of our legal indebtedness, which stood against us and condemned us; he has taken it away, nailing it to the cross."[16] Through Christ's **substitution** on our behalf, our sins are forgiven! For many of us, this is our dominant understanding of what was accomplished on the cross, because substitution has been the most common expression of the gospel since the Reformation.

Here we see that on the cross Jesus not only won the victory over evil but also functioned as our substitute, forgiving our sins and canceling the charges leveled against us. He did for us what we couldn't do for ourselves. The charges against us were too great for us to overcome. The sin we've committed had created a wall of separation between us and our heavenly Father, who is also the judge. We were created to be connected to him in Covenantal relationship, but it has been severed through sin, and there's nothing we can do to repair the damage and cross the chasm.

The consequences must be given, but the judge allows a **substitute** to receive the penalty of our sins and transgressions, and grants us mercy and forgiveness. Suddenly, all that separated us has been removed, and once again, we can function in Covenantal relationship with our Father and His

....

[16] Colossians 2:13-14

family. This is the **substitution** aspect of the gospel of Jesus: that our sins can be forgiven, and we can come back into a life-giving covenantal relationship with our Father in heaven through the death and resurrection of Jesus. There is forgiveness in Christ! You don't need to pay God back; He simply forgives you and welcomes you back with open arms as a member of His family. This is truly good news for those struggling with alienation from God and others through sin.

EMBRACING THE FULLNESS OF THE GOSPEL

The full-orbed, biblical gospel, then, incorporates **substitution** and **victory**, forgiveness of sins and freedom from bondage. The problem is that we usually emphasize one at the expense of the other, and thus end up with a "miniature" gospel that can't do everything it's supposed to do. We need to learn to express the gospel in its Covenantal aspect of **substitution** and its Kingdom aspect of **victory**. Look at it this way:

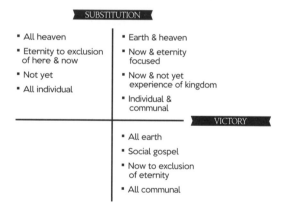

As we explore MCs, we need to embrace and live out this full picture of the gospel. What does it mean for a family on mission to have **substitution** and **victory** at the heart of what they are doing? To believe and live out *forgiveness* and *freedom*?

As an example, if there is conflict in our community, we don't try to sweep it under the rug or try to avoid it. No, we engage in it biblically (Matthew 18:15-35), seeking to bring reconciliation and forgiveness for everyone involved, because this is what God has done for us in Christ. This is expressing an implication of the gospel of **substitution**, the good news that we can be brought back into relationship with God and one another through forgiveness. Likewise, if people in our community are sick, we don't just shrug and hope they get better soon. No, we rally around them as a family with healing prayer, seeking God's **victory** over sickness for them. Why? Because Jesus defeated sickness on the cross, and we want the completeness of heaven to visit earth today (just as Jesus taught us to pray).

As we live out and incarnate the gospel, we also need to be ready to "give an answer to everyone who asks you to give the reason for the hope you have" (1 Peter 3:15). We need to be ready to tell someone the good news when the opportunity arises, with gentleness and respect, of course, but also with clarity and boldness. But there's a challenge for us here: **When was the last time someone asked you to give the reason for the hope (or faith or love) you have?** It's easy to become consumed by coming up with answers to questions that nobody is asking, rather than focusing on living authentically faithful lives in close enough proximity to people who might actually ask us some questions about the hope we have!

WHEN WAS THE last time someone asked you to give the reason for the hope you have?

What would it look like to express the gospel to those you are reaching out to through the lens of **substitution**? Through the lens of **victory**?

We need to be ready to do both, depending on the situation at hand, because people who don't know Jesus yet are going to be drawn more to one or the other. **People's "front door" into salvation will usually be either the good news of substitution or the good news of victory, and in the process of** *discipleship* **they will come to embrace both.**

TWO PICTURES OF SHARING THE GOSPEL

Perhaps the best way to give you a larger imagination for what this could look like is to offer a couple of examples of advertisements that function as windows to the longing in our culture that connects to the gospel. These advertisements appeal to the desire that seems to be embedded in everyone's heart for Covenant community and Kingdom mission.

The first ad is a commercial that Walmart and Coca-Cola put together for the holiday season a few years ago. We see a young man happily walking through his house handing out drinks to all the different people he has invited over for a party. As he walks through the house, he sings:

> The holidays are here again,
> So I'm inviting all my friends.
> The people who are close to me,
> They're my extended family.
>
> You've got my mom, my sis, my brother,
> My surprisingly cool stepmother.
> And the two kids that she had
> Before she ever met my dad.
>
> Next you got my aunts and cousins,
> They showed up with several dozen
> Friends of theirs, it's fine with me
> I've got enough for all.
>
> Here in the hall you've got my office mates,
> My best friend and his online date.
> They've all come here to celebrate.
> This is my family.
>
> My judo coach, my allergist,
> My MySpace friends and Twitter list.
> The first girl that I ever kissed
> You're beautiful, I love you.
>
> 'Cause there's one truth I have found
> And it's never let me down
> When you stock up on joy,
> There's enough to 'round.
>
> Joy, enough to go 'round
> Enough to go 'round
> Enough to go 'round and around
> And around and around...[17]

---

[17] To see this ad online, go to http://vimeo.com/33548978

Isn't that remarkable? "They're my extended family." Everyone who sees that ad wants to be in that house, because it speaks to a hunger people have for belonging in an extended family. The message of the ad (which of course we are not endorsing!) is that a big box retailer and a soda can somehow create a family with "enough joy to 'round." But even though it can't deliver on what it's promising, the ad represents an articulation of a "Covenant" gospel of belonging and family that people are hungry for.

Another example of an advertisement that proclaims a "gospel" of sorts (this time from the Kingdom perspective) is a television commercial for Levi's jeans. The video shows inspiring images of broken-down buildings in Braddock, Pennsylvania, that are beginning to be repaired. Over soaring symphonic music, a child recites the following words:

> We were taught how the pioneers went into the West.
> They opened their eyes and made up what things could be.
> A long time ago, things got broken here.
> People got sad and left.
> Maybe the world breaks on purpose, so we can have work to do.
> People think there aren't frontiers anymore.
> They can't see how frontiers are all around us.[18]

The advertisement ends with the words "Go Forth" on an open sky. The ad taps into the hunger people have to make a difference, to be part of a story bigger than their own, a higher purpose that gives their life meaning and direction. Again, the premise of the ad is that somehow we can obtain this by wearing a certain brand of jeans, which is silly. But it represents an articulation of a "Kingdom" gospel, the good news that we can find meaning and purpose in giving ourselves over to something bigger than ourselves.

YOU CAN BE PART OF God's family and have a role in the family's mission.

How do we say yes to that invitation? We become disciples of Jesus.

Ultimately, MCs exist to draw people into life in Christ, so the end game of our evangelism is discipleship, not just conversion. The gospel we proclaim is that

---

[18] To see this ad online, go to http://www.youtube.com/watch?v=2YyvOGKu6ds

anyone can receive a new life with God (Covenant) and learn to represent Him to others (Kingdom). You can be part of God's family and have a role in the family's mission.

How do we say yes to that invitation? **We become disciples of Jesus.**
MCs are simply families on mission who are following Jesus together, telling others "all about this new life" (Acts 5:20), and inviting others to follow Jesus with them. At the end of the day, MCs are **gospel communities**, where the good news of Jesus is embodied and proclaimed. They are **Jesus communities**, where people are trained to follow Jesus together, becoming the **body of Christ**, expressing the ministry of Jesus to those around. Evangelism is simply inviting people to join us as we do this.

As you think about the gospel, think about your own immediate family or network of relationships: Do you embrace one aspect over the other? What would it look like to live more fully in the gospel? What would "good news" look like to the people in your mission context? How can you begin today to move in the direction of more fully embodying the good news of Jesus in its Covenantal and Kingdom aspects? We need to ask ourselves these important foundational questions as we seek to cultivate Covenantal extended families with Kingdom mission.

4

∾ FINDING THE ∾ PERSON OF PEACE

Thus far, we have mentioned two key foundational elements of a Missional Community out of the four:

1) MCs are Communities of Discipleship (building a **discipling culture** at the core).

2) MCs are Communities of Good News (embodying and proclaiming the **gospel**).

A third foundational principle is understanding and practicing Jesus' **Person of Peace strategy** for evangelism, and letting the rhythm of your MC flow from your relationships with the **People of Peace** you find. It is difficult to overstate how important this is.

Jesus lays out this strategy in Luke 10:1-16, instructing 72 disciples in how to prepare people in the towns and villages he was about to visit.[19] A central part of his strategy was for them to center their ministry around a **Person of Peace** (translated "a person who promotes peace" in the NIV). The Person of Peace was someone who welcomed these disciples of Jesus into his or her home, was open to the message they were bringing, and served them. Once you find one of these people, Jesus says, "stay there, eating and drinking whatever they give you...do not move around from house to house" (Luke 10:7).[20]

---

[19] There are similar passages in Luke 9 and Matthew 10.

[20] You can find a much more detailed outline of Jesus' strategy in our book *Building a Discipling Culture*.

We encourage people to begin using this strategy by simply observing their normal lives. As you go about your life, look for people who know you're a follower of Jesus and welcome you, listen to you, are open to you, and seek to serve you in some way. They are interested in you and what you're "all about." They know you're a Christian and are open to you and your mission, and often find ways of serving you or your community (i.e., watching the kids during a church event, cleaning up after a neighborhood barbecue, giving you gifts of some kind).

These are People of Peace.

For example, one woman we know met a Person of Peace for the first time while walking her dog. She simply struck up a conversation with another dog-walker and found some areas of common interest in community, which turned into several more conversations over coffee. Eventually, the Person of Peace offered her expertise in business to help the church build community. That's a Person of Peace: welcoming her, listening to her, and serving her.

The thing about the Person of Peace strategy is that it's not simply pragmatic. That is, it's not just a convenient way to find people to disciple. **It's actually a way of noticing what God is already doing in your mission context.** Here's why: A Person of Peace isn't just someone who likes *you*. Jesus told us, "Whoever listens to you listens to me," so, if we are representing Jesus, these are people who are actually **showing us that they are interested in Jesus!** They are people in whom God has already been working, preparing their hearts for the good news of Jesus. So we "stay with them" because, in doing so, we are joining in with what God is doing in their lives, cooperating with the Holy Spirit. **Finding a Person of Peace means discovering where God is already at work in the neighborhood or network of relationships you're seeking to reach.**

FINDING A
Person of Peace means discovering where God is already at work in the neighborhood or network of relationships you're seeking to reach.

The first step is *always* to identify the People of Peace in whatever neighborhood or network we are seeking to reach. Then, we "stay there," as Jesus said, finding ways to intentionally spend time *as a community* with these People of Peace, sensitively exposing them to various "Kingdom experiences" (joy in community, kindness, service, fun, testimonies of God's work in our lives, meals together, prayer and worship times, etc.). You simply invite them into what you're doing as a community. Then, when they start to ask questions about it, you explain to them what's going on: In the words of Jesus, "The kingdom of God has come near to you!" In other words, we explain their experience by announcing the good news: "God is close to you, and he loves you. You can begin a new life with him in his Kingdom by trusting Jesus. Come and follow Jesus with us!"

When we really begin to understand how God works through People of Peace, evangelism actually becomes much easier than we often think it is.

"Discovering the Person of Peace principle was the most freeing thing for me," said an MC leader from the Midwest. "I realized I had been avoiding evangelism because of hurtful experiences in the past. But now the pressure is off me and my ability to convince people. I feel free to just look for the person God is already preparing!"

Here's the genius of Jesus: His evangelization strategy is *fun*.

Essentially, his "big plan" is to hang out with people who like you and then answer their questions when God moves in their lives. The refreshing thing about this is that mission becomes something we do "along the way," in the context of our normal interactions with co-workers, friends, and neighbors, instead of an additional task to cram into our already busy lives. Find the people around you in whom God is already working and join God there!

It's not complicated. It really is that simple.

This is important because sometimes MCs lock in their rhythms and gatherings with little thought to who the People of Peace are in their lives, which can actually inadvertently lead to scheduling gatherings and activities that *exclude* the People of Peace God is trying to reveal. MCs end up spending a lot of time doing "good" things at the expense of things that would help them connect as a community to their People of Peace. **This is why an MC's first priority should be to find the People of Peace God is preparing in the neighborhood or network of relationships the MCs are seeking to reach.** After you've discovered the People of Peace, you'll see more clearly how God is at work in your mission context and know better what kind of rhythms to engage in next.

Generally speaking, your MC's initial rhythms should be focused on *finding* People of Peace. Once you've found them, your rhythms should change to focus on *investing* in the People of Peace you've found, because you can see more clearly how Jesus is at work, and they will open up their whole network of people to you.

If you don't think you have a Person of Peace, you might need to get out more! Find a hobby, start playing a sport, go to the same coffee shop every day, find ways to rub shoulders with more people who aren't Christians yet, start smiling more, and saying hello to your neighbors. Find ways to become part of the fabric of the neighborhood or network you're seeking to reach. God is always at work. Most of the time, we just need to be a bit more intentional about keeping our eyes and ears open to what He wants us to do.

5

∾ BOTH ORGANIZED ∾ AND ORGANIC

We've covered three foundational principles so far:

1) MCs are Communities of Discipleship (building a **discipling culture** at the core).

2) MCs are Communities of Good News (embodying and proclaiming the **gospel**).

3) MCs find the Person of Peace (noticing where God is **already at work**).

A final foundational principle to keep in mind as you think about launching an MC is cultivating a **commitment to the *organized* and the *organic* elements** of the community's life together. Probably the biggest mistake people make in starting MCs is thinking of them primarily as events to plan or programs to run. When you plan and organize an MC in this way, the MC always ends up having an overly structured and programmatic feel, and eventually wears everyone out because it ends up feeling like more events added to an already busy week. The whole thing usually runs out of steam within a few months because it is so clunky and high maintenance.

Here's a testimony from an MC leader who made this mistake:

"In the first MC I led, we came up with what we thought was a brilliant (but complex!) plan on paper, and it was all about putting on lots of events. After about six months of lots of events, I was burned out, and so were the people in my MC. To top it off, nothing of Kingdom significance was really happening.

"It was then that I remembered a small group I had led a few years earlier. All we did was meet consistently on Thursday nights for our small group, and hang out (just for fun) with those same people quite a bit. The hanging out wasn't scheduled or planned; we just liked being with each other so we got together. Over the course of 15 months, that group grew from four people to 35 people, and a bunch of people had come to faith. I suddenly realized I had already led an MC before and didn't realize it. It also dawned on me how complicated I was making it and how event-driven it was. The reason our small group had grown so much was because we were as committed to the scheduled Thursday night as we were to hanging out on other days and being in each other's lives. We had 'accidentally' created an extended family centered on Jesus, it was infectious, and it kind of grew 'all by itself.'"

MCs *never work* if we try to "add them on" to our lives. This is often a difficult mental shift for people to make, because many of us are used to thinking of anything involving "church" primarily through the lens of events and programs. We hear about MCs, and our automatic response is to imagine them primarily as a new program the church is trying out or a new kind of event we might like to try. **MCs never really work if we treat them as programs or a series of events.**

LIFESTYLE, NOT EVENTS

We've already said that MCs are the training wheels that teach us to ride the bike of *oikos*: extended families on mission. Thus, we are talking more about the texture of a family's life together than events we attend together. **So when you think about MCs, think lifestyle, not events.**

One MC was reaching out the urban poor in a government housing project. They wore colored T-shirts and facilitated all kinds of activities at regular points in the week: cleaning up litter, helping cultivate gardens, engaging with local kids. The problem was that their interaction as a community was based solely on those events, which didn't yield a great sense of "togetherness" when they were on mission. Over time, people drifted in and out of activities, but there was never a sense of commitment or consistency to it. They were "on mission" sporadically through the events they hosted, but they weren't really a *community*. They had a firm grasp of the *organized* side of an MC, but no practice of the *organic* side.

In contrast, think for a moment about your immediate family or group of friends. You probably don't think about the time you spend with them as a succession of events you need to attend (or that you might skip if you're too busy). We don't generally tell our friends, "We already met once this week, why do we need to get together again?"

They're our friends. We enjoy getting together. We don't think of it as one more night out or as some kind of obligation we need to fulfill or an event we need to attend.

Likewise, when we think about our families, we don't think primarily in terms of the number of events per week that we attend with them. We live with them! There is a fabric to our life together that cannot be defined simply by "events." Being part of a family is a much more comprehensive and meaningful reality than simply attending events together. There is an organic "lifestyle" that we participate in together.

That's how families function.

However, in the midst of the *organic* reality of "life together," healthy families also have an *organized* element to them. In other words, family life *does* involve "events," but we think of them differently, because of the life we are living together. This dynamic shows us that there is a texture to how families function that we need to keep in mind as we think about starting an MC:

Organized   Organic

Families exist along a continuum of the *organized* and the *organic*, the *structured* and the *spontaneous* aspects of life together. For example, many families in our movement have regular, structured time together at breakfast and/or dinner, as well as other planned events such as family nights and outdoor excursions. Those organized times together are accentuated by the spontaneous interactions that take place in between those times: conversations in the hallway, interactions while cooking together, playing a game together, or simply being in the same room together with no particular activity or agenda in mind.

Think about the way many extended families do Thanksgiving dinner or Christmas gatherings together. There are *structured* aspects to it (dinner at a certain time, a game of touch football in the afternoon, opening presents before dinner, singing carols, etc.). However, there is also plenty of time for *spontaneous* interactions and just "hanging out." There are *organized* and *organic* aspects to the rhythm, and it's important for families to attend to both.

It would be odd for a family member to attend only the dinner and leave immediately afterward if no official activities were scheduled. Likewise, it would be odd for someone to skip Thanksgiving dinner because he or she were tired or just didn't feel like coming. **Being part of a family involves a commitment to the structured and the spontaneous elements of the family's life together.**

The structured times inform and feed off the spontaneous times, and vice versa. If the structured events didn't happen, the spontaneous interactions wouldn't be as rich. If the spontaneous stuff wasn't happening, the structured events would eventually feel like a chore. **Families need the *organized* and the *organic* to create the texture of life together.** MCs should have the same texture, the same balance of organized and organic elements, so they become places where people experience being an extended family on mission.

> ### FAMILIES NEED
> the *organized*
> and the *organic*
> to create the
> texture of life
> together.

Let us state it as strongly as possible:

If your MC is doing only organized events, it will fail.

If your MC is committed only to the organic "hanging out" together, it will fail.

We need a commitment to both, because the blending of the two creates a *culture* and allows our MC to grow into an *oikos*, a fully functioning extended family on mission. Here's the thing: All of us are better at one or the other. All of us have a natural leaning toward structure or spontaneity. Take a moment to reflect: What is your "default" position? Are you naturally structured? Or more naturally spontaneous? Don't just shape your MC around your natural tendency. For your MC to flourish, you'll need to intentionally lean into that which you don't express naturally. We all get to learn, grow, and become able to live in both the *organized* and *organic* facets of community life.

One of the leaders we know often talks about finding this balance for the first time:

> "We'd been talking about being committed to all aspects of the family's life. Not just the organized gathering points, but the spontaneous, spur-of-the-moment times that are always characteristic of any family. I'll never forget how one day I sent out a text to the seven or eight people we'd been investing in (the people helping us lead the MC). All it said was, 'Our family is going to Chipotle at 6 pm. Want to do dinner with us? Bring the kids and any Persons of Peace you have.' We showed up at 6 pm, and there were 45 people there. I knew we'd finally broken through [to] them [about] understanding family life together."

To achieve this, MC leaders need to help group members understand this by casting vision for a commitment to both aspects of the community's life together. Sometimes, leaders shy away from being clear about this, because they don't want to burden people, or perhaps they think that if they lower the bar, maybe more people will want to join. However, our experience has shown that MCs that start with low-bar expectations about involvement are extremely difficult to lead, because you never really feel like you are together as a family on mission. It simply becomes a succession of events that people attend if they don't have anything else going on at the time.

However, when MCs start with a strong vision for being a family on mission and high-bar expectations for commitment to the organized and the organic aspects of the MC's life, the MCs are actually quite easy to lead, because people feel like they are going somewhere together as a family, which is actually a lot of fun.

A high commitment to the *organized* and the *organic* elements of community life will be a huge help in moving your MC toward feeling like an extended family on mission. Don't hesitate to call people to this commitment!

PART 2
∽ LEADING ∽
MCs

6
⌒ VISION AND PRAYER ⌒

WHERE DO WE START?

Now that we have laid some foundational groundwork, let's move on to deal with the more practical realities of starting and leading MCs. You may find yourself tempted to skip the first few sections and jump directly to this section of the book.

We urge you not to do this!

In fact, if you have done that, please turn back now and read the earlier sections. Because there is such a wide variety of ways to structure and lead MCs, the foundational principles are extremely important to understand. You'll be using those basic principles to make on-the-ground decisions about how to structure community life and engage in mission. There is no formula or a one-size-fits-all approach. Specific *practices* cannot always be replicated in different cultures, but *principles* can always be contextualized. Because of that, it's even *more* important to make sure you understand the principles completely, so your life and MC can be an authentic presence in whatever context God places you in.

IT STARTS WITH VISION

Let's say you've read those foundational sections, and you are captivated by this vision of forming an extended family on mission together, and want to start a Missional Community.

Great.

As we said in the first section, having a clear **vision** for mission is the vital precursor to forming a community, since the missional vision is what draws people toward the community. Some of you may know immediately what neighborhood or relational network you have a heart to reach with the love of Jesus, but for others, it may not be clear immediately. How do we find this vision?

STOP, LOOK, AND LISTEN

Children are taught to "stop, look, and listen" before they cross the street. But when we think about starting an MC, too often we're like kids who forget this advice—we close our eyes and start running across the street! If you are going to start an MC, the somewhat unintuitive first step is actually to *stop*.

We need to stop because the simple answer to the question of where vision comes from is that God gives us our vision. Because of this, we cannot overstate the importance of rooting your MC adventures in **prayer**. This is where we listen to what God is saying to us, and look for what He is doing around us. It's easy for us to rely on clever ideas and quick solutions. It's easy for us to think we're smart enough, organized enough, or just plain hard-working enough to do mission successfully. When we do this, we end up asking God to bless whatever we've already put our minds to.

> **MCs CANNOT simply be a good idea or a new program. They must be rooted in vision for mission and a passion birthed in the heart of a leader though prayer.**

What we really need to do is hear from the Lord and let His Spirit show us the way. He has shaped us in particular ways, and He has already been at work, preparing the harvest fields. MCs cannot simply be a good idea or a new program. They must be rooted in **vision** for mission and a **passion** birthed in the heart of a leader though **prayer**.

One MC we know of spent nearly two years (!) simply praying that God would help them to embrace a more missional lifestyle. While we wouldn't necessarily say that time period is normative, God really touched their hearts in the process, and now they regularly bring People of Peace into the rhythms of their MC and are beginning to see people come to faith and embrace the gospel.

Consider this passage from Acts 16:6-10:

> Paul and his companions traveled throughout the region of Phrygia and Galatia, having been kept by the Holy Spirit from preaching the word in the province of Asia. When they came to the border of Mysia, they tried to enter Bithynia, but the Spirit of Jesus would not allow them to. So they passed by Mysia and went down to Troas. During the night Paul had a vision of a man of Macedonia standing and begging him, "Come over to Macedonia and help us." After Paul had seen the vision, we got ready at once to leave for Macedonia, concluding that God had called us to preach the gospel to them.

The reason Paul was traveling in the first place was because of his passion to see the good news of Jesus reach those who far away from his home base of Antioch.[21] During the course of working out this vision, it seems obvious that Paul planned to go to Mysia. But he was sensitive enough to the Spirit to know when his good idea needed to end because the Spirit had a better perspective on what doors were actually open and what was actually needed.

As we look to launch MCs, believing in the Spirit's guidance and power has to be a bedrock belief. We have to honestly believe that apart from the Spirit, we can do nothing. Our ideas, intellect, plans, and hopes are worthless if they are done without the Spirit's leading and empowering. What we've seen in America's über-entrepreneurial culture is that this lesson can be hard to learn (sometimes only the failure of an MC does it for us). In most Western cultures, where education and knowledge are idolized, setting out on the adventure of leading an MC when you don't have all the answers from the outset, when you need to make mistakes and work things out as you go, can be challenging.

If we could advise anything from the beginning, it would be to take time to seek the leading of God's Spirit for the vision of your MC and allow Him to shape where you're being sent and how the vision will incarnate itself in that context.

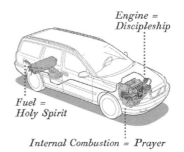

Engine = Discipleship

Fuel = Holy Spirit

Internal Combustion = Prayer

We said earlier that if the MC is the missional vehicle, then **discipleship** is the

---

[21] Acts 13:2 shows that Antioch was Paul's original sending center and home base.

engine. We might also say that the **Holy Spirit** is the fuel in the engine, and **prayer** is the internal combustion that makes the whole thing go!

The three simple questions to ask in prayer are as follows:

1) God, who are you sending us to?

Remember that we are typically called to either a *neighborhood* or a *network of relationships.* Most of the time, God reveals this to you by bringing you a Person of Peace from that neighborhood or network.

2) God, where are you already at work?

Remember that wherever God sends you, He is already there and already working (see John 5:17). Joining with what He is already doing will be much more fruitful than trying to come up with random ideas, so look for signs of God already at work around you. Most of the time, this is made known to us through a Person of Peace.

LOOK FOR SIGNS
of God already at work around you.

3) What is good news to this group of people?

Once we find the Person of Peace, we begin to ask the **gospel** question: What is the good news for this group of people? What aspect of the gospel will speak to their hearts most powerfully? How can we live out the message of Jesus and talk about Jesus effectively? In other words, how do we *show* them and *tell* them the good news of Jesus?

We often use the following questions (a "Passion Audit") to help MC leaders determine where God is calling them.

- **What are your heart's desires?** What are you passionate about? What excites you (kids, environment, people, family, healing, etc.)?

- **What is your holy discontent?** What grieves or saddens you? What do you see that makes you think "that's not fair!" (kids on street corners, litter, abuse, families breaking up, etc.)?

- **What are the opportunities?** Where are there places of grace, influence, and invitation?

- **What are the needs of the community?** Where could you be a blessing and/or good news to the local community?

- **What have you heard from God?** What has God said in the past, through Scripture and other people, about the present or the future?

As you begin to pray through those questions, and begin building the discipling culture of your MC, you will begin to see how to structure your MC in appropriate ways. If we start with **passion** and **vision for mission**, birthed in **prayer**, the logistical and detail questions become clearer.

7

✤ THREE EXAMPLES ✤

As we've said, it's impossible to give a step-by-step prescription for how an MC should operate, because the variety of mission contexts is huge. But to inspire your imagination for how an MC can start and develop over time, we want to give you three real-life examples of how it has happened. These are simply stories for you to consider and testimonies for you to think about. Each MC example is rooted in the foundational principles discussed at the beginning of this book (discipling culture, gospel communities, People of Peace, organized/organic). These examples represent different ways we have seen people go about the task of re-forming an extended family on mission, creating *oikos*. Think of them as lenses and perspectives to consider as you pray about your own vision and mission context.

EXAMPLE 1: STARTING AS A MID-SIZED GROUP (15+ PEOPLE)

One person we know started an MC by taking a somewhat cohesive community of Christians of about 20 adults (plus kids) who had a bit of history together and steadily moving them toward being an extended family on mission. There was already a fairly regular rhythm of UP, as they all attended a worship gathering together, and they had a moderate-to-fair expression of IN, mostly through informal events. The glaring weakness was the group's expression of OUT, which wasn't really happening with any intentionality.

They had trouble identifying any clear People of Peace in their lives, so the first thing the group did was add an element to their community rhythms in which they simply got OUT more, so they could meet some People of Peace! They started by talking with the staff at a local homeless shelter for women and children in their city, asking what the needs were and how they could serve in practical ways.

In conversation with the staff, they decided to start by facilitating a monthly "fun night" at the shelter. Sometimes they played board games with the residents. When the weather was nice, they played dodge ball outside with the kids, talking with their mothers as they watched the kids play. Other times, they brought a projector and watched a movie together. No matter what, they were always trying to be attentive to whether God would open a door to a Person of Peace. Eventually, they found three families at the shelter who were clear People of Peace. They were the ones who tended to engage more openly in conversation, stuck around afterward to help clean up, and were open to being prayed for if they had a need.

In addition to this very specific monthly OUT activity, the group continued to strengthen their expression of UP and IN. They began to meet Sunday mornings for a community brunch. Everyone brought food to share, and after eating together, they'd all share something they were thankful for, do a brief Bible study and discussion, and pray for each other. They were part of a larger church, where they attended a worship service once a month. These regular gathering times were augmented by informal outings that built a sense of family: going to a park together, watching football games together, celebrating birthdays and holidays together, going out to eat together, etc.

SUNDAY	MONDAY	TUESDAY	WEDNESDAY	THURSDAY	FRIDAY	SATURDAY
MC Brunch (UP/IN)						Serve @ Shelter (OUT)
Worship Service (UP)		Huddle				
MC Brunch (UP/IN)					Informal Fun Night w/POPs	
MC Brunch (UP/IN)		Huddle				

They also began a weekly Huddle for a few of the people in the MC who seemed to show leadership capacity. Leaders trained these people in the basic principles of Jesus' life, intentionally investing in them so they could grow in their character and competency as leaders. The explicit goal of this

Huddle was to train these individuals as MC leaders, by gradually increasing their responsibilities within the current MC.

So, for a season, their "normal" monthly rhythm looked something like the following chart. Keep in mind, the activities listed were only the "organized" part of their MC's life. In between, there were always a lot of informal dinners eaten together, movies seen together, parks played at together, etc.

This was their rhythm for a season, but after a while, all the People of Peace at the shelter moved out and stopped getting in touch, and no new People of Peace emerged at the shelter. So the MC decided to stop going there. It was a new season. They needed new rhythms that would allow them to find new People of Peace. They began to prayer walk the neighborhood of the MC leaders regularly, looking for People of Peace as they walked and prayed quietly. Eventually, the MC identified People of Peace from other contexts, too: a friend from work, a neighbor, kids from the neighborhood, etc. The MC invited these People of Peace into the various things they were doing together, and relationships began to form.

IT WAS A NEW season. They needed new rhythms that would allow them to find new People of Peace.

They also started a weekly "open dinner" on Wednesday nights to foster a regular time and place for people to gather and invite People of Peace. The house they hosted it at backed up to a commons area in the neighborhood that had a playground that lots of families used. When the weather was nice, the dinners often spilled out into the yard and onto the playground, which allowed for lots of conversations with other families who happened to be at the park. The MC would simply engage people in conversation, tell them about the open dinners on Wednesday nights, and see if they seemed like People of Peace.

These dinners led to lots of encounters with People of Peace, some of whom ended up joining the MC and becoming followers of Jesus. Others remained on the margins of the MC but still orbited somewhat regularly, coming to birthday parties and summer barbecues, etc. A couple who had been trained and discipled in Huddle is moving toward starting their own MC, and the community continues to operate this way, cultivating organized and organic rhythms of the MC in response to what the Spirit shows them through People of Peace, and always discipling new leaders along the way.

As the MC evolved, then, eventually their rhythms looked a bit like this:

SUNDAY	MONDAY	TUESDAY	WEDNESDAY	THURSDAY	FRIDAY	SATURDAY
MC Brunch (UP/IN)			Open Dinner w/ POPs (OUT)			Informal gatherings w/POPs
Worship Service (UP)		Huddle	Open Dinner w/ POPs (OUT)			Informal gatherings w/POPs
MC Brunch (UP/IN)			Open Dinner w/ POPs (OUT)			Informal gatherings w/POPs
MC Brunch (UP/IN)		Huddle	Open Dinner w/ POPs (OUT)			Informal gatherings w/POPs

Hopefully, this shows you that MC rhythms can (and probably should) change. As you respond to People of Peace and what God is doing in your mission context, your rhythms should reflect this. This again highlights the importance of making everything **lightweight/low maintenance**, so that you can quickly and easily change your rhythms to respond to what God is doing and saying.

EXAMPLE 2: STARTING AS A HUDDLE OR SMALL GROUP (6–12 PEOPLE)

Sometimes an MC starts when a Huddle or small group begins to "grow the family" by inviting more people to share in the discipleship and mission rhythms the MC has established.

AS THEY PRAYED and vision began to emerge, they found that they had a heart for the disadvantaged and poor in their city.

One MC we know of started this way, when three families who comprised a small group decided to go after a vision of living UP, IN, *and* OUT together. They were part of a church that had begun to cast a vision for MCs as a vehicle to enable people in the congregation to more fully live out Kingdom life within the neighborhoods and relational networks they lived in. These three families took up the challenge and began to pray about their context and what God was calling them into.

As they prayed and vision began to emerge, they found that they had a heart for the disadvantaged and poor in their city. They all lived in the suburbs, however, and therefore didn't have any natural points of contact with those they wanted to reach out to. They needed a new OUT rhythm that would enable them to come into proximity with the poor in the city.

One of the people in this burgeoning MC knew someone who worked for an organization that provided birthday parties for kids whose parents couldn't afford them. They decided to simply partner with this organization, volunteering to serve at birthday parties for the families the organization served. They did this a few times, about once a month, and as they did so, they began to invite others into what they were doing. They talked about it with others at their church, as well as neighbors and friends, Christians and non-Christians. More people began to join them. Interestingly, quite a few of the non-Christians they talked to were very interested in the work, and often came along to help out at the birthday parties. The community was starting to grow!

After they partnered with this organization for a while, they found that several of the families they were serving had become People of Peace. These "Families of Peace" were all living in the transitional housing section of a local homeless shelter, so the MC began to focus their OUT efforts on this particular shelter (following the Person of Peace principle). They did one event per month at the shelter to cultivate relationships and look for more People of Peace. Sometimes, it was a meal they all shared together. Other times, it was outdoor games the families played together. Several of the women in the MC were hairdressers and makeup artists, so they held a "Makeover Day." All the women at the shelter got makeovers while the men played games with the kids.

As they engaged OUTwardly, they were also intentional about expressing UP and IN together, in both organized and organic ways. They spent a lot of time together, hanging out, watching football games, attending kids' sporting events, etc. They also organized several six-week small-group Bible studies that people could participate in for more relational connection. Occasionally, they hosted a worship evening where they all got together to praise God in song for an extended period of time. And of course they attended worship services together most Sunday mornings. They also started a Huddle within the MC that began to intentionally train people toward future MC leadership.

Here's an example of a typical month for this MC at this time.

SUNDAY	MONDAY	TUESDAY	WEDNESDAY	THURSDAY	FRIDAY	SATURDAY
Worship Service & Huddle			Small group study			
Worship Service			Small group study			Serve @ Shelter (OUT)
Worship Service & Huddle			Small group study			
Worship Service			Small group study		Worship Evening	

They encouraged and trained the families in the MC to look for People of Peace at the shelter and begin to connect with the families they met outside the regular once-a-month OUT time. As friendships formed and relationships were cultivated, people looked for appropriate opportunities to share the gospel and invite people to follow Jesus with them. More and more people were catching the vision and joining the MC, and several people from the shelter (and unbelieving friends who just came along!) came to faith and began to be involved in the MC and the church they were part of. Quite a few people now in the church came to faith because of the MC's work. The MC that started with three families now has around 15 families in the core team, comprising around 30 adults, and more than 40 kids (big families).

As the leaders continued to lead the Huddle within the MC, they eventually noticed one couple in particular who seemed to be ready to step out and lead their own MC. Vision for mission was beginning to form in their hearts, and God was doing some great things in their life. The MC began to invest more intentionally in this couple, and as of the time of writing, this couple is developing a missional vision of their own while continuing to serve the original MC. They are on the cusp of launching their own MC, probably with several families from the current MC.

There have been tremendous challenges along the way, of course, but the Kingdom fruit is undeniable: Hope is coming regularly to a place that is usually full of despair. People are coming to faith and becoming disciples of Jesus, finding purpose in God's Kingdom and a place in God's family. Leaders are being reproduced, and new communities are starting!

EXAMPLE 3: STARTING AS ONE FAMILY ON MISSION (TWO ADULTS)

Another family we know started an MC when they moved into a new town. They started by themselves as a missionary family. We actually don't recommend that you do this unless you've led MCs before or you are an extremely outgoing evangelist-type, because it is one of the more difficult ways to start an MC. However, we offer it as an example. We'll call this couple John and Mary.

When John and Mary landed in their new town with their two young children, they simply started praying and observing, asking God:

1. What people group are you calling us to in this season?

2. Who are People of Peace who will help us accomplish this work?

In their case, the second question (a Person of Peace) answered the first question.

Mary met a young mother named Renae the very first day they arrived. They started walking with their kids together a few times a week. Renae invited Mary to her son's first birthday party, where she introduced her to 15–20 other young moms who were informally networked together. **They perceived that Renae was the gatekeeper to a group where God wanted to move.**

Mary started to intentionally build relationships with the moms in a low-key way—lunches, play dates, dinners, a trip to a local pumpkin patch, etc. Nothing formal. Just building relationships. All of the people they were meeting in this network who didn't know Jesus were young couples with kids in diapers.

They had found their mission context! By simply "staying with" the Person of Peace, they found the vision for mission that God was opening up for them.

Next, they prayed for a group of people to start discipling, using the vehicle of Huddle. Over the course of a couple of months, God sent them four couples who were dedicated Christians but

> **ALL OF THE PEOPLE they were meeting in this network who didn't know Jesus were young couples with kids in diapers. They had found their mission context!**

not actively plugged into a local church. They started meeting every other Thursday, teaching those in the Huddle the basic principles of Jesus' life (through LifeShapes), inviting them into a deeper level of accountability and relationship with God.

Without really explaining what a Missional Community was, they just started doing it, forming an extended family on mission by celebrating birthdays and baby showers, doing meals and life together. And after several months, they added a regular dinner on the Thursday nights they weren't doing Huddle. This dinner consisted of the people in the Huddle, and they all invited people they felt were People of Peace.

In the beginning, the only specific "spiritual content" at those dinners was that everyone at the dinner would share something they were thankful for, and then they blessed the food. A couple of months in, at the dinner in December, they read the Christmas story and sang carols, and then helped the kids decorate Christmas cookies. At this point, a little more than half of the people in the group probably were not Christians.

Here's where it gets really interesting. Up to this point, all they had done was create a welcoming community that functioned like an extended family, making it crystal-clear their lives were oriented around Jesus, and doing some regular and rhythmic things that pointed to Jesus.

Shortly before Christmas, three of the couples who had been coming asked about plugging into something with more spiritual content. There wasn't a lot of "structured" spiritual time up until now in their gatherings, but they had been observing John and Mary, who were open about their relationship with God, and it intrigued them. There was no 27-point plan of exactly how everything was going to go; it was simply the fruit of identifying and engaging with People of Peace and discerning how the Holy Spirit was working, and responding to those things.

In light of the new developments, John and Mary shifted the focus of their Thursday night dinners. (They changed their rhythm in light of how People of Peace were responding! See how that works?) This was the new rhythm:

- 5:30–6:30, Dinner: Anyone could come, even if they didn't want more spiritual content.

- 6:30–7:30, Bible study: a simple study and discussion that always concluded by having each person answer this question, "What is God saying to me, and what am I going to do about it in the next seven days?"

At other times in the week, John and Mary continued to have other more informal family events (corn-hole tournaments, running a 10K together in town, baby showers, etc.). This provided a place where more people could connect without the pressure of the Bible study group.

The MC was beginning to reflect the fullness of the life of Jesus (UP, IN, and OUT):

- Their UP times were the bi-weekly Huddles with the people helping them lead the MC and the biblical teaching after the Thursday dinner group, with a few worship songs on an iPod so they could sing and the little kids could sing and dance together.

- Their IN times were the Thursday dinners, but also the informal meals and things they did to feel like family, as well as corn-hole tournaments, barbecues, play dates, football games, etc. In addition, Mary and John had a family tradition of going to a local diner each Saturday morning with their kids, and they constantly invited people to join them in that family outing.

- Their OUT was initially a new concept for the people in the MC, so John and Mary spent some time helping them understand why it was important for them to invite friends who don't know Jesus. They also decided to do an OUT activity that served the disenfranchised by visiting a nursing home once a month with their kids, to visit and spend time with lonely people there. Most didn't have family living nearby, and they had no one visiting them. The residents loved having all the babies and toddlers around!

This was what the MC's monthly rhythm looked like at this time. Again, keep in mind that this doesn't include all the organic getting together that was happening in between. Also, some of the families attended a local church service, but others did not, so that happened on Sundays for some of the families.

SUNDAY	MONDAY	TUESDAY	WEDNESDAY	THURSDAY	FRIDAY	SATURDAY
Worship Service				Huddle		Breakfast at the diner
Worship Service				Dinner + Bible Study		Breakfast at the diner
Worship Service				Huddle		Nursing Home
Worship Service				Dinner + Bible Study		Breakfast at the diner

Again, this MC was started by one family who "parachuted in" among a group of people they didn't know. It grew because they attended to the different seasons of development:

1. A season of finding a few key People of Peace who opened up a wider network to them. Then, as they got to know the people in this network and built relationships with them, they found out who was open (more People of Peace).

2. A season praying for God to send people who were already Christians and were open to investment from John and Mary, who might want to help them lead the burgeoning MC.

3. A season developing those people (in Huddle) while they started doing more extended family dinners with light spiritual content.

4. A season diving deeper into spiritual content and a higher commitment to being family.

This all happened over the course of about eight months. That may feel like a long time to some of you and a short time to others, but it gives you an example of pace. Sometimes things take longer than this; sometimes they don't take as long. It all depends on what God is doing, what People of Peace He is working in, and how well we are attending to the opportunities He is giving us.

NO FORMULAS OR RECIPES

We offer these examples in the hope that they will spark some imagination and display some of the foundational principles in a concrete way. There is no "best way" to start an MC, because you need to consider circumstances and People of Peace. None of these examples is a formula or a recipe. We hope these examples will simply give you some practical considerations to think about as you pray about launching your own MC.

To give you some more "handlebars" to help in your prayer and planning, the following sections bring out some of the patterns we've seen at play in fruitful MCs (including the ones outlined above).

8

~ GROWING AND ~ MULTIPLYING

So far we've discussed the foundational principles of MCs, how to get them started on the right track, and a few real-life examples. But once an MC has gotten off the ground, how does it grow? More importantly, how do we implement the dynamics necessary to raise up new leaders and multiply new MCs? This chapter is all about giving you practical tools to grow and multiply an MC.

TWO PHASES OF RHYTHM

As you discover People of Peace in the context God is calling you to, you will begin to develop rhythms of gathering (organized and organic) that enable your MC to develop a culture and life together. We don't want to be too prescriptive in this, because there is so much variety in MCs based on mission context and People of Peace, etc. But we do want to offer a few thoughts that may be helpful as you discern a rhythm for your MC.

Because so much is determined by the People of Peace, MCs often have two distinct phases of rhythm.

Phase 1: Rhythms that help you find People of Peace.

Finding People of Peace is important, because this is how you begin to discern what God is up to. Some MCs start by teaching the core members about People of Peace for a few weeks, equipping the people in the MC to become good at identifying People of Peace in every aspect of their lives. Then the rhythms of the MC are focused mainly on finding People of Peace.

That might mean of a lot of backyard barbecues and neighborhood parties where loads of people are invited over so you can begin to see who is open to your community. It can also mean training MC members to look for People of Peace among their co-workers and neighbors. For an MC reaching out to artists, it might mean attending a lot of shows and events in the city, beginning to get to know the people, looking for People of Peace. At the same time, the MC continues to gather to pray about and process together what they are hearing and seeing as they engage in these People-of-Peace-finding rhythms. At the beginning stages, it is quite important to emphasize this kind of OUT activity (perhaps at least two to three times a month).

Phase 2: Rhythms that help you "stay with" People of Peace.

Once People of Peace are identified, the MC often shifts rhythms considerably, because Jesus told us to "stay there" once we find a Person of Peace. People of Peace reveal where God is working, and we shift our rhythms in light of this because we want to be like Jesus, who only did what he saw his Father doing (John 5:19). Often it means focusing rhythms on relating to the specific People of Peace that God has brought to the MC. For example, a neighborhood-based MC might spend a few months in the summer having a lot of People-of-Peace-finding events, and then a few months in the fall going through an Alpha course[22] with the People of Peace found in the neighborhood.

MC rhythms often function this way, swinging between seasons of **gathering new People of Peace** and then seasons of **investing in the People of Peace they find**. Seasons of planting seeds and seasons of reaping crops. In all of this, keep the triangle of UP/IN/OUT in mind. As we move OUT in finding or cultivating People of Peace, we must also be gathering UP and IN to pray and process together about what God is saying to us, as well as to be a family together. All three dimensions of the Triangle need to be strong for an MC to reflect the life of Jesus.

Overall, remember that your rhythms aren't set in stone once you establish them. Staying flexible is really vital, because you'll want to be able to respond to what God is doing and saying. It's OK to experiment and find out that something doesn't work. It's OK to change your rhythms if you find you need to adapt to a situation that has changed or simply if you tried something that didn't work. You have permission to fail. Just get up and keep going.

....

[22] Alpha is a small-group Bible study that introduces people to the Christian faith in a low-key, low-pressure way. See www.alpha.org for more info.

FIVE SIGNS OF *OIKOS*

Another pattern we've seen is that MCs that really become extended families on mission have several common elements. We call these the **Five Signs of oikos**. These five markers give us an indication that we are functioning well together as an extended family on mission. If these five things are happening fairly regularly (perhaps weekly or so), in organized or organic ways, we will be on our way to cultivating *oikos*.

1) EATING TOGETHER

Families on mission eat together a lot. There's something inherently community-fostering about sitting down at a table together, or hanging around a barbecue grill, or just talking with snacks and drinks around. We often add food to the gathering even if it isn't at a prescribed mealtime. It's worth the preparation and cleanup required.

2) PLAYING TOGETHER

Families on mission laugh together a lot because they are often having fun. It should be fun to belong to the family. All purpose and no play make for a dull MC! Make sure you're playing as hard as you're working.

3) GOING ON MISSION TOGETHER

Families on mission have a mission, obviously, so they are often engaging in mission together, in organized events as well as informal conversations. All play and no purpose make for a pointless MC! Make sure people know why you exist as a community.

4) PRAYING TOGETHER

Families on mission pray and worship together regularly, reading Scripture and listening to God together, because our connection to Jesus and one another is what makes our MC something worth belonging to.

5) SHARING RESOURCES

Families on mission share their resources. This doesn't necessarily mean we have a common purse, but there is some degree of sharing our resources with one another, because this is what families do. This might be people sharing a lawnmower, or pitching in to help someone pay an unexpected medical bill, or simply bringing food to share when we eat together. There is something about economic sharing that fosters a sense of family.

Here's the way one MC did it:

> "My wife and I led an MC together that was focused on young families. Money was really tight for all of us at the time. One of the things we began to do was to think about what it might look like to help each other financially. Of course, that's hard to do when *everyone* is struggling financially. But what we began to do was schedule our meals together a month in advance and buy groceries in bulk together. Some meals we'd all eat together, some we'd eat separately, some meals we'd make way too much of and bring to other people's houses (and then they'd do that for us on other nights). Each family saved hundreds of dollars each month on groceries, but what was more amazing was the sense of family and togetherness it brought to our group. Even people who weren't Christians yet were noticing what we were doing and wanting to get in on it."

Another MC we know all have keys to each other's houses so people can have kids over to play, find a quiet place to study or retreat, or use the larger spaces for parties. They are not only sharing resources but also sharing People of Peace! Some of the families in this MC also share a car and intentionally look for opportunities to use their finances to help one another take missional adventures.

PEOPLE FALL into one of two ditches: They either over-program their MC, making it feel like a series of events, or they don't meet enough because they don't want to "burden" people.

KEEP IT SIMPLE

It's easy to feel overwhelmed when thinking about the rhythm of your MC, and because of this, we find that people fall into one of two ditches: They either **over-program** their MC, making it feel like a series of events, or they **don't meet enough** because they don't want to "burden" people. Ironically, the latter ends up making the MC again feel like a series of events, just less frequent (and poorly attended) ones. Neither ditch actually creates a sense of extended family.

We encourage you to think in terms of a commitment to the organized/ structured aspects of a family's life and the organic/spontaneous aspects. Think in terms of simple, repeatable patterns, and then review regularly to see which "ditch" (too organized or too organic) your MC is closer to. Ask questions about MC members' engagement, participation, and enjoyment of the MC. This will help you make lots of small corrections as you go rather than making massive changes every once in a while.

Remember the simple monthly chart for each example we gave of MCs? Those patterns are simple and repeatable.

Make things simple, begin living in the rhythm of it, and simply invite others to join you. Change things up if it's not working. **Be careful to be consistent for long enough to give the rhythms enough time to take effect.** Sometimes the key to breakthrough is simply to keep being consistent, because the most important changes can be the subtlest.

Engage in the rhythms that seem best as you pray and listen, and be patient with the process. Sometimes MC leaders tend to get bored with the regularity and repetitive nature of food, fun, mission, prayer, and sharing together and are tempted to "spice things up" for the sake of variety. We urge you not to succumb to this temptation! Families are built on rhythm and routine, not shock and awe. Create simple, repeatable, lightweight, low-maintenance rhythms and then simply work the plan. Engage consistently in the rhythms and build a sense of *oikos*—being an extended family on mission. This will be quite counter-cultural to our "quick-fix, instant" society, where we expect everything to be astonishingly successful in just a few months! Take your time and grow your MC slowly, deeply, and authentically.

SOWING, REAPING, AND KEEPING

Let us share another pattern we've found to be helpful in giving a picture of the kinds of "family gatherings" your MC could have to help people get to know Jesus and your community in a low-key way.

The concepts we talk about in this section are largely taken from a book called *Sowing, Reaping and Keeping* by Laurence Singlehurst. The picture gives you a window into a process we often observe in people outside the faith who experience Christian community through an MC and eventually come to faith in Jesus and maturity in discipleship. It's not a prescriptive or normative process, meaning that it doesn't necessarily *need* to happen this way. But it is a description of how it *often* works as People of Peace go from the fringes of an MC to full-fledged disciples of Jesus.

The overall progression is fairly simple and can be seen in Jesus' parable of the sower (Matthew 13:1-9):

1. **Sowing Stage.** The seeds of the gospel are sown to many people, with varying degrees of depth.

2. **Reaping Stage.** In some people's hearts, the gospel seed sprouts and grows, and they respond and decide to follow Jesus and step more into life in God's Kingdom.

3. **Keeping Stage.** The people who have decided to follow Jesus continue to grow deeper roots as they join the discipleship rhythms of the MC, becoming more mature, and they begin to sow and reap with the others in the community.

Again, there are exceptions that we should always be open to, but generally speaking, this is a picture of the relational process by which People of Peace go from being disconnected from God and community to being fully integrated into God's Kingdom and community life as a disciple of Jesus. They meet people who know Jesus, they see God's power at work, they experience the overflow of Christian community, and eventually, they hear the good news of Jesus and respond to it.

Here is a diagram of this process:

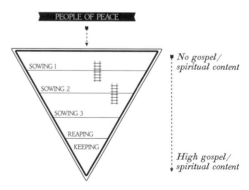

Two things to note about this diagram: There are more people at the top of the triangle than at the bottom, because as the gospel/spiritual content increases, the number of people involved decreases. Again, this doesn't necessarily *need* to happen; it's simply a description of how it *often* does happen in our experience (and, incidentally, what we notice in the life of Jesus).

Now let's talk about what it all means! First comes sowing. You'll notice we have three "stages" of sowing, numbered one, two, and three.

SOWING 1 (S1)

In this stage, People of Peace generally interact with you and the MC on a purely relational level. They probably know you are Christians and perhaps that you "go to church together" (you never want to be secretive about your faith). In this kind of environment, there isn't any official, programmed gospel/spiritual content (unless someone asks, of course). You want people to walk away thinking:

- "I like those people!"
- "Maybe God is good."
- "These Christians are fun to be around. There is something different about them."

Our friend Hugh Halter has said, "Sometimes I wonder if evangelism is simply defying people's expectations of Christians."[23] That's often what S1 is all about. People of Peace are simply rubbing shoulders with your *oikos* and are surprised that they actually like hanging out with you and your "friends from church," and would love to do so again sometime in the near future.

EXAMPLES OF S1

Remember the commitment to organized and organic? Often, the best S1 events are simply the organic times your MC is just "hanging out."

- Dinner with you and few friends from the MC
- Watching football with a few people from the MC
- A trip to the park with folks from the MC
- Catching a movie with a few people from the MC

Notice that each has a "with a few people from the MC" clause. One of the simplest but most powerful things you can do to welcome People of Peace is to **bring others from the MC into your interactions**. Instead of just connecting individually with People of Peace, bring others along! Something

---

[23] Hugh Halter and Matt Smay's book *The Tangible Kingdom* is all about how to do this.

about letting them see you interact with other Christians usually has a much more profound impact than if you meet with them individually.

Here are some other examples, on the more "organized," all-MC level:

- A big party where everyone from the MC invites their People of Peace
- A camping trip with the MC and People of Peace
- A game of family kickball at a local park where everyone in the MC invites their People of Peace

Essentially, S1 is about creating space where people can connect relationally in low-key ways.

SOWING 2 (S2)

The second stage of sowing is still very heavily relational, but adds a little bit of gospel/spiritual content (emphasis on the "little" part—no sermons here). The goal is that people experience everything they do at an S1 event but are also observing something more explicitly spiritual that your MC is engaging in.

EXAMPLES of S2

Here are a few examples of S2 events.

- A meal with the MC and People of Peace where, before eating together, all share something they are thankful for and then say a prayer for the food.
- A story time with a few friends at a local bookstore where the books being read have some kind of spiritual content and People of Peace are joining with their kids.
- Watching a movie and talking about the spiritual implications with a few people—everyone can join in, nothing is off-limits, and people can say whatever they want.

IN THE S2 PHASE,

stories and personal narratives are the most compelling gospel/ spiritual content.

- A meal with the MC and People of Peace where everyone shares their "highs and lows" from the day. People from the MC can share what God has been doing in their lives lately.

Often in the S2 phase, stories and personal narratives are the most compelling gospel/spiritual content, because they don't feel contrived or programmed. People simply share about what God is actually doing in their lives, what He has been saying to them lately, etc. The People of Peace walk away thinking, "Wow! Their faith actually means something to them, and it's actually affecting how they live their lives and the kinds of people they are. Interesting!"

You'll notice on our diagram that there is a bridge from S1 to S2 (and from S2 to S3). This is important to understand. The bridge represents **trust**. When people go from S1 to S2, *they need to know they are doing so.* In other words, you don't want to surprise them with the spiritual content of the gathering you are inviting them to. If they have been to a S1 event and are expecting the same kind of thing, hearing gospel/spiritual content will often feel like a "bait and switch" if you're not careful, and you will

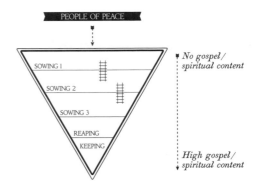

have burned the "bridge of trust." Don't burn that bridge if you can help it! Make sure people know what they are being invited to.

For example, if you are inviting a Person of Peace to come to a gathering with your MC where you hand out street survival kits to the homeless, you might say something like this:

> "Hey, I know you've done some fundraising for the homeless before, and I thought you might like to join me and a few friends this Saturday morning. We're handing out street survival kits to homeless folks and just hanging out with them, drinking coffee, nothing too crazy. Oh, and FYI, usually when we go down there, we offer to pray for some of the homeless guys who've had a hard week. Obviously, you wouldn't have to pray for anyone, but I just wanted to give you a heads-up. Sound OK?"

It doesn't need to be a big thing—you just want to make sure they know what's going to happen ahead of time and give them the opportunity to say, "No, thank you," if it makes them uncomfortable. Not everyone will move from

S1 to S2 at the same speed, and often, you'll burn the bridge of trust if you end up surprising people with spiritual content they aren't expecting.

SOWING 3 (S3)

Up until this point, we have simply let people "taste and see." They have experienced and observed Christian community. They have perhaps heard people pray or give a testimony of what God has done in their lives recently. But there hasn't been any overt sharing of the gospel yet. This shouldn't make us uncomfortable, because it's the pattern we see in Jesus' ministry: **He let people experience the Kingdom before he explained the Kingdom.**

JESUS LET PEOPLE **experience the Kingdom before** he *explained* **the Kingdom.**

If we think back to the Person of Peace framework in Luke 10, we realize that People of Peace don't hear an explanation of the good news from the very beginning. First, they simply experienced the good news ("heal the sick who are there"), and then they were given the explanation ("the Kingdom of God has come near to you"). People experienced and tasted the goodness and power of God, and then the gospel was shared. Experience before explanation.

This is essentially what is happening with our People of Peace in S1 and S2, if they spend enough time there. They are experiencing the goodness of God through community and enjoying some of the "fringe benefits" of Christian community simply by being around a Kingdom-seeking community. (Incidentally, this is why it is so important to have a healthy balance of UP, IN, and OUT. We want to be living out and experiencing the things we are inviting people into.)

S3 is where they hear the *explanation* of the *experience* they've had. They simply hear the gospel, but generally are not asked to give a response (yet). They are given an opportunity to hear the good news and process it, ask questions, and let the implications sink in more deeply. Once again, there must be a bridge of trust from S2 to S3 so people know what they are walking into and aren't surprised by the level of spiritual content.

EXAMPLES OF S3

Here are some examples of S3 events:

- A Christmas Eve service. Often, these quite moving, beautiful services end up preaching the gospel without an awkward or forced response time afterward.

- A conversation you have with a Person of Peace that naturally leads to talking about the gospel because of the questions he or she asks. "Always be ready to give the reason for the hope you have" (1 Peter 3:15). Incidentally, sharing the gospel informally is a great skill to train your MC in.

- Celebrating Easter as an MC in someone's home and sharing the Easter story and its true meaning.

- A neighborhood Vacation Bible School that your MC hosts at someone's house during the summer. (This is a fun, incarnational approach to VBS that is catching on in many places around the United States right now.)

Again, notice that these examples cover a wide variety of circumstances across the organized/organic continuum, from full-blown programs like VBS to informal and spontaneous conversations.

REAPING

The reaping stage is not much different from S3. The difference is that, while S3 is a presentation of the gospel without the expectation of response, the Reaping Stage is about actually inviting the Person of Peace to respond to the gospel and become a disciple of Jesus. Usually at this point, the Person of Peace is a regular attendee and participant in your MC and knows what you are all about and won't be surprised by this invitation. He or she has already heard it and is still coming back for more, which should tell you something!

The Reaping Stage is when the seed that has been sown has taken root in good soil, has been watered and nourished, and is now growing and ready to be harvested.

EXAMPLES OF REAPING

Here are some examples of reaping:

- At the end of a conversation with a few friends from the MC, you ask the Person of Peace if he or she wants to join you in following Jesus intentionally.

- You MC goes on a two-day retreat full of fun, laughing, relaxing, teaching, and worship followed by a chance for all to share what God has been saying to them and what they're going to do in response.

- You have simply shared the gospel with your Person of Peace, and he or she is clearly ready to respond right then. Grab the opportunity! Don't assume the person needs time if it seems like the Holy Spirit is moving in his or her heart in the moment (even if it's at an S1 event).

KEEPING

It's not enough to have someone make a "decision" for Christ or pray a prayer. Our commission is to **make disciples**, so this is always our goal in proclaiming the gospel. We want these People of Peace to become disciples of Jesus. This means they simply join us in the MC as we "do our thing." They learn to follow Jesus as they join your family on mission and do what you do (because you have a **discipling culture** at the core of your MC). They'll begin to discern their own People of Peace and walk them through the same process, while growing in their character and competency as disciples of Jesus as they serve and lead in the MC.

> **IT'S NOT ENOUGH to have someone make a "decision" for Christ or pray a prayer. Our commission is to make disciples.**

In other words, "getting across the line" isn't enough. We want to *keep* them in the Kingdom and grow them to maturity as disciples of Jesus so they are fruitful, "attaining to the whole measure of the fullness of Christ."[24] We are making disciples who can make more disciples, not simply seeking converts.

EVANGELISM AS A COMMUNITY

The beauty of doing evangelism this way is that everyone in the MC plays a role. There's a place for the extrovert, the introvert, the eloquent, the stuttering, the social butterfly, and the awkward. Some people will be amazing party planners. Others will be great at leading others in a short meditation on Scripture. Others will be wonderfully gracious hosts for dinners. Still others will be excellent at attending to all the details that need to happen to pull off a great barbecue. Others will be great networkers, inviting many people into the community. Growing the family (which is all evangelism is) becomes a community endeavor! We

----

[24] Ephesians 4:13

take the People of Peace we have as individuals and introduce them to an entire community, and people have a chance to experience "church" as a network of relationships instead of a meeting to attend.

One person might start a relationship with neighbors, but as she build relationships with them and invites them to meet the whole MC in formal and informal ways, someone else entirely ends up sharing the gospel with them. Cool! Some people may be great at planning and hosting incredible parties (S1); others may not be as good at that but are very sensitive to knowing when people may be ready to hear an insightful spiritual remark (S2) or perhaps even sharing the gospel in a warm, welcoming way (S3). Everybody gets to play a role in an MC when we attend to the various phases of sowing, reaping, and keeping.

LEADERSHIP AND MULTIPLICATION

One final pattern of each MC example above is that each one had some kind of leadership pipeline in place. The **discipling culture** that existed "below the surface" of the MC meant that more and more leaders could be trained as they were living as an extended family on mission. This is important to highlight because the only way to truly multiply an MC is by raising up leaders with vision to *launch new Kingdom ventures*.

New MCs won't start simply because you have willing volunteers. The MCs need to be led by *leaders with vision*, and the way to get leaders with vision is to **disciple** them into being able to do the things you're doing. Since it takes

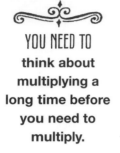

a while to really disciple someone well, you need to think about multiplying a long time before you need to multiply.

If you're thinking about multiplication only when it's time to multiply, it's too late.

We consistently hear from leaders that they are surprised at how much time and effort it takes to disciple and raise up new leaders. One MC leader remarked that she knew discipling new leaders is the right thing to do but was challenged by how long it was taking. She has to continually remind herself of the vision of making disciples and remember to invest in the process at God's pace! She actually developed a few key phrases and Scriptures to rehearse when she is tired or frustrated. That's the kind of intentionality it takes to truly multiply an MC.

Kingdom leaders don't just appear the moment you need them, and they don't emerge from a six-week class. They have to be cultivated through discipleship, and it takes a while to disciple someone well. **Part of building a discipling culture is having multiplication in the DNA of the community from the very beginning.**

Remember our metaphor: MCs are a great vehicle that gets you to the missional places God is calling you to go, but *discipleship is the engine.* Without a process of discipleship for raising up leaders within the MC, your vehicle might look good, but it's going nowhere. Having a process of discipleship that actually works is vital to being able to go to the land of Kingdom multiplication.

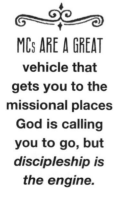

So during the entire process of launching and leading an MC, you're always doing two things at once:

1. Doing it, and

2. Training others to do it.

This is the pattern of Jesus. He was always training his disciples to do the same things he did. So as you lead, you're always raising up new leaders. As you engage in mission, you're always raising up new missionaries. It means always having an eye on training others to do the things we're learning to do ourselves. Healthy multiplication happens only if you have quality leaders, and you get quality leaders only by being intentional about raising them up. They don't get it simply by osmosis—you need to train them. Having a healthy, accountable leader with vision is the rate-determining step for multiplication. **This means that multiplication will never go faster than leadership development. You will never multiply your MC faster than you raise up new leaders who can do what you do.**

YOU WILL NEVER multiply your MC faster than you raise up new leaders who can do what you do.

This is why identifying potential leaders and starting a Huddle within your MC early in the process is important. Huddle is the vehicle that trains new leaders within an MC, and the MC is, of course, simply the extended family on mission together that provides the context for training those in Huddle. This is how MCs and Huddles "fit together" in the larger paradigm of discipleship and mission.

When it does come time to multiply your MC, make sure that *vision* is the reason for multiplication. MCs operate and multiply best in a **low-control, high-accountability** environment, where leaders listen to God themselves and come up with a vision but are well supported and equipped to lead in an accountable and responsible way.

Sometimes MCs multiply by essentially splitting in two, with one half going with the new leader who's been raised up and the other half staying in the current MC (which usually is heading into a new season of mission). Other times, MCs multiply by a leader taking a few people from the current MC and "hiving off" to form a new MC based on their vision, from which they'll also gather others. Other times, one of the small groups within the MC is sent out to gather people and create a new MC.

Any way you multiply, remember that none of it happens unless you are discipling leaders as you lead your MC.[25]

....

[25] Our book *Multiplying Missional Leaders* is all about developing a consistent process for discipling and reproducing leaders.

PART 3

~ PRACTICAL ~
TIPS

9
～ WHY MCs FAIL ～

As we work with leaders all over the world who are launching MCs, we are asked all kinds of "nuts and bolts" questions. This section includes the best help we can give when it comes to some of the practical issues of launching and leading MCs.

WHY DO MISSIONAL COMMUNITIES FAIL?

The first practical issue to address is the common mistakes MC leaders make. Not every MC is successful! In fact, many fail in one way or another. As we talk with leaders, the following seem to be the top 10 reasons MCs don't make it.

1) THE MC LEADER DOESN'T KNOW HOW TO DISCIPLE THE OTHER LEADERS IN THE MC.

This can result in a few different outcomes:

- The MC becomes merely a miniature version of the culture the leader is trying to bring God's Kingdom into. The leader doesn't know how to disciple people to be missionaries to a culture; therefore, they never truly learn how to be "in the world but not of it." Instead, they are "in the world and of it," more influenced by the culture than influencing and redeeming the culture. There is a lot more cultural relevance than there is Jesus.

- Another outcome of an MC leader not discipling people well is that the MC becomes a "religious space" that is all about who is in and who is out. Doctrine is used as a weapon of defense instead of something that helps to describe the reality and inherent goodness of God's Kingdom. People who don't know Jesus find the MC the equivalent of running into a brick wall. In this case, there is a lot more law than there is Jesus.

- One final possible outcome of a discipleship-less MC is that, if people do become Christians, there is no one to disciple them, because neither the MC leader nor the other leaders in the group know how to do it. New believers become stagnant, the life they were told about in the gospel never comes to fruition, they become disenfranchised, and divisions within the MC start to occur.

2) THE MC LACKS A CLEAR MISSION VISION.

The vision of every MC in the world could say something like, "We exist to love God, love people, and serve the world." The problem is that this isn't a specific enough vision for an MC, because no MC can actually love and serve *all* the people in the world. The point is finding a "crevice" of society where a gospel presence is lacking and forming a Jesus community there. It's not generic and broad—it's specific and focused. If you never truly identify the specific neighborhood or relational network God has called you to, or if you don't do the things necessary to incarnate the gospel in those places, it'll be very difficult to sustain, grow, or multiply the MC.

For example, one of the MCs we've worked with focused on artists in a certain city. This is a very clear vision for a specific network of relationships, which is good. However, the people leading the MC were part of a unique subculture, and many of the activities the MC commonly enjoyed and practiced resonated with others in that unique subculture but not necessarily with *artists*. The MC ended up behaving like it was for people from the unique subculture, but saying that it was for artists. The group found itself stuck in the middle, unable to grow or gain momentum. In the end, *neither* artists *nor* people from the unique subculture found a place of family within this MC. In this case, the leader needed to decide: Does this group exist for artists or the unique subculture we are part of? The leader needed to make the vision clear and act on it.

3) THE MC IS NOT LAUNCHED WITH ENOUGH PEOPLE.

One critical mistake many MCs make is launching with fewer than 12–15 adults in the core group. Why is this important? Because an MC needs to be an "extended family" and adopt the social dynamics of a group that size. Mission works so well with this size group because new people who don't know Jesus are welcome to hang out, observe, and form relationships, but they can also be semi-anonymous if they choose. Because the group is larger than a typical small group, new people don't feel uncomfortable if they don't fully participate or are simply in observation mode when the "family" has spiritual time together. There is a kind of "gravitational pull" to groups this size that tends to bring people in.

If you have fewer than 12–15 adults, you'll almost inevitably default to the social dynamics of a small group (six to 12 people total). In this kind of group, everyone shares, things get very personal, and it tends to be focused inward. This is not a bad thing in and of itself, but the problem is that it's not generally a comfortable environment for someone who doesn't know Jesus. We've found that when the group gets to 12–15 adults, there is a shift in these dynamics toward a more "extended family" atmosphere. It's very difficult to grow into this kind of atmosphere if you start with a "small group" atmosphere.

> AN MC NEEDS TO be an "extended family" and adopt the social dynamics of a group that size.

That being said, one of the example MCs we discussed above started with just one family. However, this family had led a few MCs before and knew very well how to gather people, along with the social dynamics they were shooting for. So, the exceptions to the "15 adults" rule are:

1) if you are an outstanding gatherer of people, and/or

2) you're a veteran MC leader who has done this a few times, seen them grow and multiply, and know what you're doing already. If this is your first rodeo, so to speak, we recommend you follow the general rule of trying to gather at least 15 adults around your vision before launching your MC.

4) THE MC ISN'T PART OF A LARGER WORSHIPING BODY.

Many times, people get excited about MCs and decide to simply start one that isn't connected to a larger worshiping body (a central church). We understand this impulse, but the reality is that life on the missional frontier isn't easy. It's an incredibly amazing adventure, worth every ounce of prayer and effort you put into it, but it is hard.

Because of this, it's important for MCs to be connected to a wider church body, accountable to and supported by others, and regularly cycling in to a worship service with a larger group (75+ people) at least once a month. This is where MCs will be reminded that they are part of a bigger story, hear how God is working in other places, hear teaching and preaching for the wider community, take communion together, and worship with one unified voice.

The scattered church gathers so that it can scatter well. One of the reasons we gather together is to keep mission sustainable. A church that only gathers and never scatters tends to get "overweight," not working off the spiritual calories they are taking in. But a church that only scatters and doesn't gather enough tends to get faint and out of breath, because it isn't taking in enough calories to sustain the energy they are pouring out. In our experience, MCs that operate alone eventually wither and fall off the vine because it's generally too hard to sustain apart from a wider community. (Church plants can sometimes get around this dynamic, but in many cases they struggle as well.)

5) THE MC LEADERS AREN'T ACCOUNTABLE.

MCs are built on the principle of **low-control** *and* **high-accountability**. Some MC leaders love the low-control part, but don't really like the high-accountability part. If MC leaders aren't willing to be held accountable to the vision God has given them, it is a spiritual problem, a discipleship issue. MCs are not an excuse for rebellious renegades to finally have a chance to do things their way. The Great Commission is simply too important for us to be weak on this point.

If someone you are discipling refuses to be accountable to leadership, he or she can't be an MC leader, because eventually, whatever is toxic in that person that refuses to submit to someone in authority will seep into the rest of the group, and the toxicity will spread. Be clear about the expectations regarding accountability and make sure to follow through on those expectations.

6) THERE IS TOO LITTLE MISSION, PARTICULARLY AT THE START OF THE GROUP.

If your MC is just starting, we recommend you do *much more* mission (OUT) than worship and teaching (UP) or hangout time for people already in the group (IN). You need to be out in your mission context participating in activities that help you identify and connect with People of Peace, and then spending a lot of time with them. If mission doesn't get into the DNA of your community early on, it is nearly impossible to include later without essentially restarting the MC. This has to be modeled by the MC leaders and core group—you cannot tell people to do what you're not doing and go where you're not going.

> **IF MISSION**
> doesn't get into
> the DNA of your
> community early
> on, it is nearly
> impossible to
> include later.

From a pragmatic standpoint, perhaps you could think of it this way: For the first three or four months, every time you do something UP- or IN-focused, do at least two or three things that reflect an OUT-focused mission.

This struggle is very common. One MC we know recently disbanded and went back to the drawing board for this reason. They started with conversing, having fun, and building community and figured they'd get to the mission part once they were good enough friends. But their testimony was that the MC "felt good" but never really had the life in it that they wanted. The MC started "looking sideways" at each other instead of upward to God and outward to the world. They were all IN, no OUT or UP. They disbanded it to invest in a season of looking upward and outward first.

7) THE MC LEADER DOES EVERYTHING.

MC leaders who try to do everything for the community eventually burn out, which is usually the end of the MC. Another problem with MC leaders doing everything is that it negates one of the most powerful elements of an MC: the fact that they are small enough for *everyone* to participate and contribute meaningfully. As our MCs begin to facilitate true *oikos*, they begin to essentially function as "little churches," which is essentially the way the early church operated.

For example, the instructions Paul gives in 1 Corinthians chapters 10–14 are essentially principles for how an MC-sized community would gather, function, and participate together.[26] It's clear from those passages that *everyone participating* was a big value, and this is one of the main ways MCs distinguish themselves from worship services. In an MC, everyone brings something (food, a word of encouragement, a prayer, a song, etc.). Make sure that everyone in your MC feels like he or she has an opportunity to participate and contribute meaningfully to the community and that you as the leader are not just doing everything for everybody.

One little way to delegate responsibility is to do what one MC leader did: When someone new came to their gathering, the MC leader showed them around the place and introduced them to a few people. Then she said, "On your first night, we'll show you where everything is. Next time around, if there's someone new, can you show them around and introduce them to a few people?"

Another easy way to delegate is to make sure that everyone shares in the "family chores." If there is a mess in the kitchen after a community meal, everyone helps clean up. One MC said they had a stated value for the whole MC to leave a house cleaner than how they found it. This way hosting an MC gathering can feel like a blessing and not a chore.

8) THE MC MIMICS A WORSHIP SERVICE OR SMALL GROUP.

This is a common mistake, usually made when people don't keep in mind that an MC is really just an extended family on mission together. We are building a family, not just planning events. It's easy to make this mistake, however, because most of the time a worship service or small group is the main Christian gathering that people have been part of, so they automatically adopt one of those as the standard. But it doesn't really work. MCs that are basically smaller church services don't work, and neither do MCs that are basically large

---

[26] The church in Corinth likely had, at most, 60 people in it when Paul wrote this letter.

small groups. The gatherings will feel a little "off," and visitors typically won't stick. It will be difficult to maintain momentum, and eventually, everyone will get tired.

When different numbers of people are in the room, different sociological dynamics are at play. Sociologically speaking, worship services are essentially an expression of **public space**, MCs are an expression of **social space**, and small groups are an expression of **personal space**.

- **Public space** is where people connect through an outside influence, like watching a football game or attending a lecture, or going to a church service. This space generally works with 75 or more people.

- **Social space** is more like a house party, or backyard barbecue, or art gallery opening, where we can informally interact with others. This space generally works with 20–50 people.

- **Personal space** is where people connect a little more deeply, like at a small dinner gathering or discussion group. This space generally works with six to 12 people.[27]

Essentially trying to mimic a worship service in your MC is attempting to have public space dynamics with social space numbers. It just doesn't work. It seems that you just can't cheat this! It's like a law of nature. So don't make your MC gatherings into little worship services.

9) THE MC DOESN'T DO EVANGELISM.

In the past few years, many people have seen evangelism done poorly, with a lot of manipulation and arm-twisting. Therefore, they are leery of sharing the good news of the Kingdom for fear of being associated with "those people." In addition, evangelicals (lately, though not historically) have lacked an expression of the gospel as it pertains to social justice and inequity. (Thankfully, many

....

[27] For more information, see E.T. Hall's work on proxemics or Joseph Myers' book *The Search to Belong*.

evangelicals are re-embracing the rightful place of embodying the good news of Jesus by standing against injustice, etc.)

That said, one of the problems is that MCs can go ditch to ditch, in other words, going from "All evangelism/No social justice" to "All social justice/No evangelism."

Some hope that people will come into the Kingdom purely because of the love they experience in Christian community, touting the phrase "Preach the gospel at all times; if necessary use words" (which, incidentally, St. Francis never actually said or believed). From a biblical perspective, words *are* necessary. "And how can they believe in the one of whom they have not heard? And how can they hear without someone preaching to them?" (Romans 10:14). The gospel cannot only be implied—it must be proclaimed!

We need to reclaim evangelism as a vital part of our MC. Part of the task will be training people in what the gospel actually is, and another part will simply be us getting over ourselves enough to stop worrying about how others perceive us.

If your MC is heavily involved with social justice (sex trafficking, homelessness, racial issues, poverty, etc.), make sure that evangelism is also a key part of your strategy, so that you're operating in the fullness of the good news. People in MCs need to have the capability of sharing the gospel with others. We recommend you re-read Chapter 3 on the gospel (page 23) and think deeply about ways you can train your MC in relational evangelism.

10) THE MC DOESN'T ENGAGE WITH THE SUPERNATURAL.

We're not talking about blindly embracing some of the crazier manifestations of supernatural ministry here. However, if your MC is not good at praying, listening to the voice of God, and engaging with the presence, leading, *and power* of the Holy Spirit, your MC will ultimately fail to thrive. Try to imagine the early church thriving without the Holy Spirit at the forefront. We must be willing to learn how to engage with the supernatural aspects of the Holy Spirit's ministry if our MCs are going to be more than just social clubs or do-gooder societies.

These are the top 10 reasons we've seen MCs fail. But we want to leave you with one more thought: **Not every MC makes it, even if you attended to all of the reasons above. And that's OK.** Paul failed as much as he succeeded. Remember the goal is to build a family on mission, an *oikos*, and MCs are simply the training wheels that help you get there. A single MC that fails is, in and of itself, no big deal. If yours fails, learn as much as you can from what happened, take a season of rest, listen for fresh vision from the Holy Spirit, **and have another go at it**.

Remember Jesus' parable of the sower: We are simply scattering seeds and looking for good soil. It's not like modern agriculture, where there are tidy rows, and everything bears fruit in a uniform pattern. Leading MCs (and life generally!) is just not like that.

10
～ FAQ OF MCs ～

We work with leaders all over the world who are launching and leading MCs, and we get a lot of questions! In this chapter we answer some of the most common questions and issues that people have when it comes to the practical realities of leading a extended family on mission.

WHAT IF WE CAN'T FIND PEOPLE OF PEACE?

One common issue in MCs is the struggle to find People of Peace. Some MCs seem to hit a wall when it comes to connecting with people outside faith in Jesus. What can you do about this?

First, as we said above, if you are having trouble identifying People of Peace, you may just need to get out more! Find a hobby, make a habit of going to places where people hang out, or whatever. Just get out there and see what God might show you.

However, there are sometimes other hindrances to finding People of Peace. One issue we have identified is the willingness to "out" yourself as a follower of Jesus by identifying yourself with him as his disciple. **When Jesus sent the disciples out in Luke 10, he sent them out to *represent him*.** They were to go into the villages *in the name of Jesus*, under his banner, as his representatives. He told them that, as they did that, they would experience welcome and rejection. He took away their excuses and comfort and all the things they normally depended on (they were sent out as "sheep among wolves"). He gave them instructions on what to do when they were welcomed and when they were not welcomed. He made it clear that to go out on this mission was to "out" yourself as a follower of Jesus, and see how people responded.

TO FIND A PERSON
of Peace you need to be willing to risk finding a Person of Unpeace.

Some will receive you. Others will reject you. Or worse. Until we're ready to face that, we won't find a Person of Peace.

In other words, to find a Person of Peace you need to be willing to risk finding a Person of Unpeace.

There's a difference between being sent out with the authority of Jesus and just hanging out with people. Jesus' disciples weren't wandering into random towns pretending they were travelers. They had been sent out by Jesus as those who were in a relationship with him—going to certain places in his name, representing him, with a specific message to proclaim and task to perform. Jesus didn't send them out as undercover agents. They were openly proclaiming that God's Kingdom had come near in Jesus. There was nothing subtle about why they were in town.

We hesitate to fully "out" ourselves as disciples of Jesus for all kinds of reasons. Perhaps we don't want to be associated with aggressive street preachers or certain TV or political personalities. Perhaps we are scared of what people might think or say about us. Perhaps we just don't want to be rejected. When we hesitate, we are happy to show kindness and demonstrate the love of Christ to others in many ways, but we become tongue-tied and quiet when it comes to sharing the content of our faith, because we don't want to be lumped in with "those people." We have allowed their "proclamation without presence" to push us into "presence without proclamation." We need presence *and* proclamation for effective witness.

Take a look at the matrix below:

High Presence

	SHOW, DON'T TELL	SHOW & TELL	
Low Proclamation	• Embodied but not explained • Way of life with no words • "Nice" community, no transformation	• Embodied and explained • Way of life matches words shared • Kingdom breakthrough	*High Proclamation*
	DON'T SHOW, DON'T TELL	TELL, DON'T SHOW	
	• Not embodied or explained • No words, no way of life • Spiritual apathy	• Explained but not embodied • Words with no way of life • Hypocrisy, judgmental	

Low Presence

Some of us are prone to being **presence-oriented** in our evangelism, valuing the building of relationships with nonbelievers above all else. We'll need to lean into the **proclamation** aspect of evangelism, learning to actually share the good news with others. Others of us are prone to being **proclamation-oriented** in our evangelism, eagerly desiring nonbelievers to hear the gospel above all else. We'll need to lean into the **presence** aspect of evangelism, learning to live out our faith authentically and cultivate real relationships with nonbelievers.

When you go out representing Jesus (in his name, with his authority), then what Jesus says is true of you: "If they welcome you, they welcome me. If they reject you, they reject me." If you are ashamed of Jesus or the gospel in any way, if you are unwilling to experience the same kind of scorn and opposition that Jesus faced, you won't be able to perceive the Person of Peace, because that person is primed and ready to receive Jesus, and you won't look like Jesus to him or her, because you are essentially going out "in your own name."

Not on behalf of Christ.

There seems to be a line we must cross, a death we must die before we can see People of Peace. When we die to ourselves and embrace being identified as a "fool for Christ," we will find People of Peace, and we'll also find rejection and opposition, because you don't get one without the other. The good news, though, is that if we embrace this and truly go out in Christ's name, then his authority will clothe us, and his power will protect us and flow through us.

If we're having trouble identifying People of Peace, we must ask ourselves: Are we willing to cross the line and risk the scorn of the world so we can recognize Persons of Peace and thus join Jesus in restoring and healing people's lives? We need to be if we're going to join God in his work in our neighborhoods and relational networks.

WHAT DOES A TYPICAL GATHERING LOOK LIKE?

As you've probably noticed from the examples we gave above of different ways to start an MC, the way to start an MC varies. The same is true of a typical MC gathering. Remember, it is about **principles, not practices**.

Rather than come up with a formula for you to follow, we'd rather you simply start experimenting and see what works for your context and vision. Use the principles outlined in the first part of the book, and be sure to include a good mix of community, prayer, mission, and training, all through the lens of UP, IN, and OUT. (And food. Always have food if possible.) Anything that honors Christ and falls within this vision is legitimate.

Because we know that concrete examples can be helpful, here are a few ideas to kick-start your creativity. Your OUT times will be dictated by your vision for mission, obviously, so the following suggestions and ideas are mainly aimed at UP/IN type gatherings, where the people in your MC meet together to grow closer to God and one another and pray into their missional context.

A gathering might include the following:

- Food (sharing a meal together is best)
- Socializing, having fun, laughing, playing
- Sharing communion together
- Storytelling (testimonies), particularly about things we are thanking God for
- Praise and worship to God
- Prayer for healing or for other needs in the MC
- Reading and reflecting on Scripture together
- Praying for the mission context you are reaching out to
- Planning upcoming events

As we said earlier, your MC will also do OUT together in specifically missional activities, serving and witnessing to the missional context to which you are called. These events need to happen regularly so they are seen as an integral part of the community's life. We encourage you to go on mission together from the very outset of the MC's life. Don't wait until group members get to know each other better. Our experience is that if you don't start with mission right away, it's difficult to add it later. Moreover, the MCs that gel the fastest are actually the ones whose members go out on mission together right away, because they share common "battle stories" from the missional escapades they have been on together (the successful and the not-so-successful).

WHAT ABOUT KIDS?

For MCs that have children involved (which is most of them that we've seen), kids are almost always one of the first issues people ask about. What do we do with the kids? How do they fit into this thing we're doing?

The overarching principle to keep in mind here is that MCs are the training wheels that help us ride the bike of *oikos*; MCs cultivate a sense of being an extended family on mission! **In other words, we're not trying to plan a slick production—we're trying to build a family. And families have kids in them.**

In a family, sometimes the kids and adults are together doing a "grown-up thing," such as dinner or evening devotions. Sometimes the kids and adults are together doing a "kid thing," such as a birthday party or decorating Christmas cookies. And sometimes the kids and adults are doing separate but related things, such as the kids playing games in the basement while the adults talk upstairs after dinner.

Before we offer a few examples, we'd like to highlight the larger issue. Because we are trying to build extended families with Kingdom mission, not just run a program or figure out what to do with the kids, the question really shouldn't be, "How are we going to *deal with* the kids?" It should be, **"How are we going to disciple our kids well?"**

THE QUESTION really shouldn't be, "How are we going to deal with the kids?" It should be, "How are we going to disciple our kids well?"

Ultimately, this is the responsibility and challenge of the parents in the MC, alongside the MC leader (with equipping and resourcing from church staff). The question for parents in the MC needs to shift from "Who will disciple my kids?" to "How will I disciple my kids?" The kids who are part of the community are *just as much* in need of equipping and discipling as the adults are. There are various ways to accomplish this, but we must remember that we are not figuring out what to do with kids in an MC. We are **intentionally raising them as disciples of Jesus**. This puts a lot of things in perspective.

One lens that may be helpful in thinking about discipling kids in MCs is thinking through the three basic environments in which people learn: **Classroom**, **Apprenticeship**, and **Immersion**.

1. **Classroom.** You learn by hearing a teacher/lecturer pass on facts, data, and information. This is very familiar to us because the Western educational system is built on this method of learning. Whether in elementary school or college, we are expected to absorb what is presented to us in a lecture. Similarly, much of the Bible and the basics of faith are taught to kids this way.

2. **Apprenticeship.** You learn to do something by coming alongside someone who does it well, observing him or her, and eventually doing what he or she is doing. If you want to be a surgeon, you apprentice yourself to a surgeon after medical school and enter a residency. You learn by having the instructor *show* you how to do something, and then by eventually practicing it yourself, with feedback from the instructor. For example, rather than only *telling* children how to pray, we *show* them how to pray by doing it with them, and having them try it alongside us.

3. **Immersion.** You learn to do things by being immersed in the culture. All children learn to speak their native language fluently without any formal lessons at all. They learn simply by being immersed in a culture where people speak the language. They pick it up almost by osmosis. When our kids are immersed in a vibrant culture of Christ-like love and community, they pick up the behavior, language, nuances, and depths of that community simply by being immersed in the life of the community.

Each form of learning has strengths and limitations, but what sociologists have discovered is that the best learning happens when there is a dynamic interplay among all three at one time: What is being taught in the classroom environment is being modeled in the apprenticeship environment, with all of it being reinforced and given depth and meaning and nuance through immersion in a culture that is congruent with what is being taught and modeled. The most powerful formative environment for kids (and adults, of course) is one where faith is both **taught *and* caught**.

As you think and pray about how to form the kids in your MC as disciples of Jesus, think about what you could do in these different environments.

Classroom: Teaching Bible stories, basic Christian doctrine, the story of Scripture, etc. Often children's ministry programs are great for this.

Apprenticeship: Watching how the adults in the MC live out the story of Scripture, learning from parents and other adults in the MC how to pray, express thanksgiving, forgive those who hurt you, pray for the sick, lead in worship, clean up afterward, serve others in the MC, etc.

Immersion: It is crucial that the MC fosters and sustains a discipling culture in which the community actively believes (and therefore practices) the things they talk about. Kids pick up a *lot* by simply being part of a vibrant Christian community.

Some very interesting research shows that this kind of environment actually provides kids with the very best chance of maintaining a lifelong vibrant faith into adulthood. In a decades-long study, researchers examined the factors that went into kids growing up with and maintaining a vibrant faith. The highest two correlations had to do with observing parents living out their faith, which we might expect. But the third highest correlation (far higher than youth group or Sunday school) was simply whether kids had an opportunity to observe their parents living out their faith with other adults. Kids who observe real faith in their parents and other adults in the community tend to grow up with the same faith.[28]

Now that we've emphasized the overarching principle of *discipling* our children well (instead of just dealing with them), we've found that the best MCs have a mixture of **all three** of the types of gatherings we mentioned:

The Coffee Shop: Together doing "adult stuff," with kids participating. This might be a gathering where everyone eats together, everyone shares something he or she is thankful for, someone leads some worship songs, everyone reads the Scripture, and everyone takes communion. The kids are involved in the whole thing.

The Kids Party: Together doing "kid stuff," with adults participating. This might be a gathering where you celebrate all the kids' birthdays for

---

[28] We are almost certain that this research came from a study conducted by the International Mission Board (http://www.imb.org) but were unable to locate the specifics of the research before printing.

the month in the MC. The games and activities are all geared to children, but all the adults participate and help facilitate the party and get to speak blessing over the kids.

The School: Separately doing parallel things. This might be a gathering where, after eating together, someone teaches a lesson in the basement with the kids while the adults gather in small groups upstairs to share with each other and pray together. Or perhaps the kids go outside for supervised play while the adults discuss plans for the next outreach event the MC is planning.

> **WE HAVE OFTEN been surprised by how deeply the experience of being consistently included in a family on mission imprints itself on a child's soul.**

The bottom line is that there is no one right way to work with the kids in your MC. We encourage you to experiment with involving the kids in different aspects of community life, letting them participate and contribute in their own way, taking their immaturity in stride. The goal is never to have a smooth meeting with no interruptions; it is simply to cultivate an extended family on mission. Families are messy (especially when they involve kids), so don't worry if a particular gathering doesn't seem to go smoothly. Think about the bigger picture of whether the kids are learning to follow Jesus with the rest of the community. **We have often been surprised by how deeply the experience of being consistently included in a family on mission imprints itself on a child's soul.**

WHAT ABOUT BAPTISMS, FUNERALS, WEDDINGS, ETC.?

When it comes to important rites of passage like baptisms, weddings, and funerals, each church needs to work out which events can be held in MCs and which ones need to be more centrally anchored, according to the church's tradition, context, and resources. Here are some general thoughts on a few of the more common rites of passage, based on our experience and observation.

BAPTISMS and BABY DEDICATIONS

We have seen some churches release and resource people to do baby dedications and baptisms within their MCs. This allows the event to be more personal for the candidates and their families. These events can also function as great OUT events. Other churches prefer to use baptisms and dedications as opportunities to bring the whole church together to celebrate what God is doing.

WEDDINGS

MCs often function as great places for people to meet and start dating, and then a wonderful environment within which to prepare for marriage! When a couple who has been involved in an MC begins to prepare for their wedding, the MC is often highly involved in the wedding. We see many MC leaders asked to participate in leading the wedding ceremony. The MC provides a wonderful environment for the couple to grow in their marriage after the wedding. Which makes sense, because they're simply extended families on mission!

DEATH, BEREAVEMENT, and FUNERALS

When MC members suffer bereavements, often the MC is the first line of support, since it is the primary environment in which they are loved and known, and can be practically cared for. Although helping someone who is grieving the loss of a loved one can feel daunting, the simple things can make the most difference: Putting together a sign-up sheet for people to provide meals, cleaning the house, going with the family to meet with funeral directors and lawyers, helping them walk through practical decision-making, etc. These things make a tremendous difference to people in the MC who are suffering bereavements. We have often seen an MC do a *better* job than a pastor could in supporting people through these situations.

Of course, there are situations in which an MC cannot handle the weight of the loss by itself, and needs the support of the wider church leaders or staff. However, if handled well, times of bereavement can actually be an extremely powerful and significant time for an MC. You really begin to feel like family when you grieve together and support one another in times of deepest need.

WHAT ABOUT PASTORAL CARE?

Whenever possible, we recommend that issues of pastoral care be dealt with first within the MC. This is part of what makes MCs not simply events but actual communities, authentic expressions of the Body of Christ. This provides an opportunity for people to love and minister to one another in practical ways. For example, with a little equipping and training, visiting with and praying for the sick can easily take place entirely within the MC.

We also encourage MCs to send members of their community (especially those with a pastoral gifting) to prayer ministry or pastoral training courses, to enable them to grow in their ability to pray and care for one another.

However, some pastoral situations are too difficult to deal with at the MC level. MC leaders should never hesitate to get leaders from the wider church involved if they feel an issue is too complex or difficult to deal with themselves.

WHAT ABOUT MONEY AND OFFERINGS?

How is money handled in an MC? There isn't necessarily a right way to do this, but in our experience, the model we outline below seems to yield the best results.

We think about giving through the lens of **tithe and offering**. The tithe is the regular, rhythmic, consistent giving of 10 percent of our income to the work of the Kingdom. We use it as a general rule of thumb when talking with people about their plan for giving. An **offering**, then, is anything beyond the tithe that we want to offer to God in some way.

We recommend that the tithe go to the central church, because this is what creates the space, training, equipping, and support for the MCs to exist and thrive. This helps to foster an attitude within an MC that says, "we're all in this together," instead of, "it's all about us." Giving to a central church reminds us that our MC is part of a larger whole.

(A related word about tithing: We highly recommend that one of the ways you disciple people in your MC is to move them toward tithing via automatic bank draft. We believe this is the very best way to be intentional and accountable with your giving, instead of sporadic and private. There is no better way to be intentional than to set up something that happens automatically!)

Beyond the tithe, offerings can happen within the MC as needs and opportunities come up. For example, perhaps someone in the MC needs money for rent or a mortgage payment. Instead of sending him or her to a centralized church benevolence fund, it is entirely appropriate for people within the MC to give money to this person to help pay his or her rent (like any family would). This is money that is given above and beyond the regular tithe, and offerings are taken at the discretion of the MC leader.

What about MCs having budgets from central church funds? In general, 95 percent of MCs don't need these kinds of budgets. Remember, MCs are extended families on mission together. Most of the needs can simply be met organically as the MC seeks to move out in mission together, with everyone pitching in. The one exception is MCs that are reaching the marginalized or poor. Sometimes, the weight of the mission requires more resources than can be provided for by the core MC team. In this case, it would be appropriate for a church to give an MC a budget out of the central fund.

WHAT ABOUT FOOD?

As you've probably noticed, we think it's really important!

There is something about sitting down at a table with others to eat together that has been fostering a sense of community and family since the dawn of human history. So we highly recommend having some kind of food at every MC gathering you have. It really is that important.

AS YOU'VE probably noticed, we think food is really important!

However, it's also important to note that you should not make all the food yourself. You are not a restaurant owner serving customers. You are cultivating a family on mission, and in a family, everyone contributes. Set up a schedule for others to bring snacks so you are sharing the burden as a community. When you eat full meals together, have everyone bring something to share, enough to feed their family plus a little more so there's an abundance. Remember, hospitality is different from "entertaining." You are not putting on a show or providing a service—you are part of a family having a meal together.

Also, ask and expect people to help you clean up afterward. Again, this is a family on mission, so everyone has "chores" that help the family function. A common tactic we use is to simply ask a specific person to do a specific task: "Martha, could you put these chairs back in the garage? Thanks! Roger, can you help me load the dishwasher? Thanks!" It's easy to fall into a "hospitality" mindset where we feel the house has to be spotless before people come over, and then we need to clean up after everyone. But that's not how families function together. So make sure you have people show up early to help you set up and stay after to help you clean up. These things are just as much a part of the gathering as any other part.

HOW BIG SHOULD A MISSIONAL COMMUNITY BE?

In the first section, we said that a Missional Community is 20–40 people, but those aren't hard figures. A good size for an MC depends on many different factors, from the size of the spaces you're meeting in to the culture of the place you live to the capacity of the leader of the MC.

For example, urban MCs tend to be smaller than suburban MCs, mainly because the spaces they are meeting in are smaller. In the United Kingdom, MCs tend to be more in the 18–30 person range. In suburban America, we've seen MCs have as many as 60 people. It all depends. Part of your responsibility as an MC leader is to discern where the lid[29] for the MC is, and make sure you are discipling people into leadership so you can multiply once you hit that lid.

In general, MCs need to be mid-sized, which means they are larger than a small group but smaller than a whole church congregation. A general figure to shoot for as a minimum would be 12–15 adults, plus any accompanying kids. If an MC has fewer than 12 adults, the group tends to take on the feel of a small group, which means sustaining long-term missional activity will be difficult because you won't be "big enough to dare."

HOW DO WE HANDLE CONFLICT?

When dealing with hurt or conflict, we believe in applying literally the principles outlined in Matthew 18:15-35. This means addressing issues

---

[29] The "lid" is the number that, once you hit it, you can't seem to get past. It's like someone is putting a lid on your growth as a community.

quickly and directly first with the person with whom there is an issue, and seeking reconciliation and forgiveness above all else. Encourage community members to practice this prayerfully and with respect and gentleness. If the issue is not resolved following open dialogue between the people concerned, the MC leader may need to step in as a neutral mediator to help facilitate resolution. If the matter remains unresolved, it should be taken to a member of the church leadership team.

One of the ways MC leaders can facilitate a Matthew 18:15 culture is by refusing to entertain accusations or problems with others in the MC that people bring to them, unless the person bringing the problem has already spoken with the person he or he has an issue with. This is how we can model biblical conflict resolution and forgiveness for those in our MC. When we practice this consistently, it's amazing how the culture of an MC starts to feel like a place of peace and safety for everyone. It's worth being a "stickler" about Matthew 18:15.

IT'S WORTH BEING **a "stickler" about Matthew 18:15.**

WHAT ABOUT MISSIONAL COMMUNITIES IN THE INNER CITY?

Here are a few quick tips if you're starting an MC in an inner-city minority neighborhood (especially if you're not a member of that minority group).

Don't send in a bunch of white people. Just because you have a lot of people who are willing to be part of this MC doesn't mean they all should stream in together. In our experience, *four people* at the most (plus any kids) should move into a neighborhood initially. For many reasons (most of them deserved), minorities have a difficult time trusting middle-class white people. Don't put up barriers if you can avoid it. If a brigade of white people comes marching into the neighborhood, they will be met with distrust and unease, because it will communicate arrogance.

Find the Person of Peace. Who is the person embedded in the neighborhood you are seeking to reach who lives there, who is trusted by people there, who can serve as the gatekeeper to the neighborhood? When you find this Person of Peace, they should be fully involved in the life of the community as they are in relationship with you and journeying toward Jesus. As they comes to faith, the Person of Peace should be part of the leadership of the MC. Ultimately, the leader needs to be someone who "looks like" the neighborhood. When Paul preached the gospel in Philippi (Acts 16), Lydia responded to the message and was the Person of Peace, a leader who "looked like" a person from Philippi, who could function as a gatekeeper to the wider city.

Don't come up with something new. When you're trying to find the Person of Peace, don't try to come up with a new program or plan for the community. Chances are there are already a few community groups focused on this neighborhood. Join up with them. Remember, you're looking for just *one* important relationship. But also remember that finding the right person can take some time. In our experience, it can take six to 12 months to find the first Person of Peace relationship.

Don't plan what your MC will look like ahead of time. You don't know what the MC is going to look like until you find the Person of Peace. Don't try to come up with a silver bullet plan to save the community. Ask questions of people—don't provide answers. Stop, look, and listen to the people and the neighborhood. Find out where God is already at work. The Person of Peace and those close to him or her, with your coaching, will be the ones who shape the rhythm of the MC.

Be consistent and commit for the long haul. Communities in poor, urban areas do not change overnight. Urban sociologists say it usually takes two generations for lasting change to remain. By most church program standards, that's a long time! It doesn't mean that your MC needs to commit to the neighborhood for 50 years, but it does mean you need to have realistic expectations and be prepared to commit consistently and patiently for a good length of time to see something started.

Obviously, there is a lot to think about with inner-city MCs, but we think these are the some of the most important things to think about at the outset. The Holy Spirit can make up for some mistakes you make along the way, but we recommend not deviating from these principles.

HOW DOES MY FIVEFOLD GIFTING AFFECT MISSIONAL COMMUNITIES?

Depending on your base gifting from Ephesians 4 (which shows how each of us is created as either an Apostle, Prophet, Evangelist, Pastor or Teacher), you will lead your MC differently from other people with a different base gift.[30] In other words, if you're an Apostle, the way you start, lead, sustain, and multiply your MC will be quite different from someone who is a Teacher, for example. (Which is as it should be!)

Here are some of our observations about how each gift base tends to lead MCs.

APOSTLES

Apostles are **future-oriented**. Their fundamental question is, **"Are we leading the people of God to their destiny?"**

Apostle-led MCs usually are highly magnetic to many different people, orbiting around the leader, who typically has a lot of charisma and the ability to gather others. Frequently, Apostle-led groups grow the quickest. Their mode of multiplication is often to split down the middle because of the pressure of the speed of growth. Mature Apostles should put their energy and effort into discipling new leaders well, and grow the skills to manage such a maneuver (as long as they are discipling new leaders within the MC), even though it can be fraught with pastoral landmines, as multiplying an MC can be relationally difficult for some.

PROPHETS

Prophets are **integrity and justice-oriented**. Their fundamental question is, **"Are the people of God hearing His voice and actually responding?"**

Prophets tend to focus on the mission, but are not quite as evangelistic as other types. Prophets often implement a high-visibility approach, since they desire a more radically incarnational approach to presenting the gospel. This means that they and their groups tend to be quite radical, with high demands placed upon members. For example, if you know an MC in a tough urban context where there is lots of talk and action about reclaiming the city by their very presence and engagement with the people out on the streets, it is probably an MC with strong prophetic leadership. Such groups can grow by multiplying, but they often keep the core team and allow new work to bud off into a new context.

....

[30] For more on "Fivefold Gifting," see *Building a Discipling Culture* and http://fivefoldsurvey.com.

EVANGELISTS

Evangelists are **new-life-oriented**. Their fundamental question is, **"Are more people entering the Kingdom of God?"**

Usually, Evangelists love to go straight after People of Peace in their chosen mission context. Evangelists identify the gatekeepers to that place and stay with them to invest in them. You often see Evangelists literally going out in pairs, finding some People of Peace, building relationships, and through them reaching a whole neighborhood that was previously unreached. Eventually, Evangelists look to hand the group on and go into a new context or send out others in twos to do similar work elsewhere.

TEACHERS

Teachers are **truth-oriented**. Their fundamental question is, **"Are the people of God immersing themselves in Scripture and incarnating it?"**

Teachers often go into an existing context where the witness for Christ is struggling or almost extinguished. They will give themselves in modeling how to live the Christian life, whether in worship, community, or mission. Mature Teachers do this with a great deal of humility, so it won't even feel like teaching much of the time. They tend to stay for a lengthy season, but many will eventually begin to look for a fresh context requiring their help and then hand over their group. Teachers send out new groups who will be characterized by having been thoroughly prepared with a clear model of how to do things. Teachers like models!

PASTORS

Pastors are **transformation-oriented**. Their fundamental question is, **"Are the people of God seeing transformation, healing, and redemption?"**

Pastors long to bring transformation to people and communities by establishing and building on long-term relationships. Pastors highly value the integrity of becoming fully embedded in their context. This means that although things are not as spectacular at first, Pastors have a long burn approach to mission that can be remarkably transformative over the course of a few years. We have noticed that this model works especially well in the suburbs. Because relationships are at the heart of everything Pastors do, it can be more difficult for them to multiply MCs, but they do find it easier to grow as a "bud" or "shoot" off a small group of people and perhaps to take what they are doing into a neighboring area (or even neighboring street).

HOW DO WE DO A PRAYER WALK?

Prayer walking is one of the most transformational activities you can do for a neighborhood. It is also an excellent low-bar OUT activity to get your MC moving in the direction of mission. We have heard story after story of God's Kingdom breaking into a neighborhood after people from an MC had faithfully prayer walked it for a few months. It's almost as if God actually heard and answered prayer!

PRAYER WALKING is one of the most transformational activities you can do for a neighborhood.

One neighborhood-focused MC began by prayer walking their neighborhood for a few months before starting any kind of public activity. Interestingly, after prayer walking a few times, they all had a strong sense to focus their energy on one half of the neighborhood (around 90 homes). They figured this was from God, and as they did it, incredible breakthrough followed. People were inexplicably open and ready for the gospel, dozens of people came to faith, and they eventually multiplied into two MCs. It all started with a commitment to walk and pray in a neighborhood.

Here are some tips on how to do a prayer walk in your neighborhood.

Take a walk around your neighborhood, either in small groups of two to four people or by yourself, and:

- Ask God to give you a sense of what He feels for the people in the neighborhood.
- Pray that the Spirit will make the Father known to the people who live there.
- Ask: What would it look like if the Father's Kingdom existed in this place like it does in heaven?
- Ask God for insight into how you can serve and love the people here in ways they can understand.

- Ask God to provide opportunities for conversation and interaction with people while you're out walking around the neighborhood.

- Stop and talk to anyone you see while you're out walking. Not, "Hey, I'm prayer walking, can I pray with you?" More of a "Hey, how are you doing today?" kind of thing.

- Ask that God give you People of Peace in the neighborhood.

- Ask for grace in everything you do as an MC.

- Most of the time, simply talk and listen to God quietly.

Afterward, take some time to either write down or discuss with others anything you noticed or heard from God as you walked. Make sure you take action on those things, and plan your next prayer walk!

CONCLUSION

~ SMALL THINGS ~
WITH GREAT LOVE

"Don't look for big things, just do small things with great love."
— Mother Teresa[31]

In 165 AD, a devastating epidemic swept through the Roman Empire. Historians don't really know what the disease was (some suspect smallpox), but one thing is certain: It was extremely lethal. The epidemic lasted 15 years and killed anywhere from a quarter to a third of the empire's population. Almost a century later, another plague ravaged the Roman world, killing massive numbers of people. It is reported that in the city of Rome alone, 500 people were dying *per day* at the height of the epidemic.[32]

In the midst of the daily horror of family members and friends dying all around, many people fled the cities and sought refuge in the countryside—especially those among the privileged classes, who had estates where they could retire until the devastation passed. The pagan priests and philosophers of the day were powerless to explain the disaster or curb its advance, so many simply ran for their lives.

These responses seem like what you would expect in a time of great disaster and upheaval. The interesting thing is that one group of people didn't leave the cities in panic. In fact, this group of people purposefully stayed in the cities to look after the sick and dying, providing whatever they could for those who were suffering, even if it was merely a decent burial once the disease took their life. These people extended care and love beyond the boundaries of family and tribe and took care of any sufferers they came across.

The remarkable people who stayed in the cities to care for those being ravaged by the epidemics were *Christians*. Many actually lost their lives while caring for others. Here's what Dionysius, the Bishop of Alexandria, wrote in an Easter letter around 260 AD, during the second epidemic:

> "Most of our brother Christians showed unbounded love and loyalty, never sparing themselves and thinking only of one another. Heedless of danger, they took charge of the sick, attending to their every need and ministering to them in Christ...Many, in nursing and

---

31 Quoted in *Mother Teresa: Come Be My Light*, by Brian Kolodiejchuk

32 A fuller account of the Christian response to these epidemics is given in Chapter 4 of Rodney Stark's remarkable book *The Rise of Christianity*.

curing others, transferred their death to themselves and died in their stead…Death in this form…seems in every way the equal of martyrdom."[33]

These early followers of Jesus weren't trying to do anything heroic or significant. They were expressing simple obedience to Jesus' command to "do to others what you would have them do to you," and living out his word that "it is more blessed to give than to receive." Because they did these small things with great love, they gave sufferers hope that stretched beyond the grave and a compelling vision to root their lives in from that point on.

It is likely that many of the sick who did recover simply became Christians and joined the communities that had nursed them back to health. Because of these kinds of dynamics, Christianity went from a marginal sect on the fringes of Jewish society to the most dominant faith of the entire Roman Empire within a few hundred years.

All because of small things done with great love.

This is ultimately what starting an MC is all about. As we learn to become an *oikos* together, our job isn't to try to do big things. It's simply to do the small' things we see around us with great love, trusting that God will take our small things and all the other small things we don't see and weave them all together into a tapestry that announces His love for humanity and calls all people to new life under God, who is making everything new.

As you step out in faith to launch and lead an MC, be encouraged! You are unleashing the same power that transformed the ancient world, and you don't need to be an expert to do it. As you simply seek to take one step of faith at a time, God will be with you to encourage you, empower you, and sustain you in mission. This is a movement of *ordinary* people expressing discipleship and mission in community and letting God do what only He can. Have fun with it!

....

[33] *Festival Letters*, quoted in Eusebius' *Ecclesiastical History*.

APPENDICES

❧ NOTES FOR ❧
CHURCH LEADERS

APPENDIX 1
⌐ IT REALLY IS ALL ABOUT ⌐ THE DISCIPLING CULTURE

BEFORE WE BEGIN...

If you are a church leader or vocational pastor reading this book, we know that you will have some additional questions and issues beyond those of a typical MC leader. In this section, we attempt to answer some of those questions, and we pray they will be helpful for you. However, we have developed a process called a Learning Community that really helps you go deeper in understanding, practicing, and implementing discipleship and mission across your entire church. It's a two-year journey involving learning immersions, retreats, coaching, training, and strategic consulting.

You can find out more about Learning Communities at our website
www.weare3dm.com.

THE KEY REALLY IS THE DISCIPLING CULTURE

One of the biggest temptations for pastors when they first begin thinking about using MCs in their church is to think of them as a new program to implement instead of the result of a new culture being cultivated. One church we know of heard about MCs by going to a *Pilgrimage Week* at St. Thomas' Church in Sheffield, England (one of the epicenters of the missional movement in the Western church), came back home, spent a few weeks casting vision and preaching about it, gathered volunteers who wanted to try it out, and launched 26 MCs at once. By and large, it was an utter failure. Only one of those original 26 MCs exists today. The rest failed. The people leading the

MCs hadn't been discipled and didn't know how to lead an MC, only how to volunteer to run programs. Thus, their first attempt at leading an MC was an outright failure, which soured them on the idea of ever trying it again. Giving people too little of the "mission virus" can actually inoculate them against it!

The story of that church is almost always what happens when churches attempt to launch MCs as a new program without building a discipling culture. We've never seen MCs bear long-term fruit unless they are built on the foundation of a discipling culture that is producing missional leaders. Think of it this way: The MCs your church launches will be the "above the surface" evidence of the necessary "below the surface" process of making disciples and training leaders. If you try to launch MCs without a foundation of a discipling culture, they will be as wobbly and unsafe as a house built without a foundation.

In contrast, if you take the time and make the sacrifices necessary to build a discipling culture, the natural by-product is a crop of missional leaders with vision for mission, and the natural by-product of a crop of missional leaders is that they start gathering people around them to fulfill the dreams God has put in their hearts, thus Missional Communities. The culture of discipleship is the ground out of which the plant of mission grows.

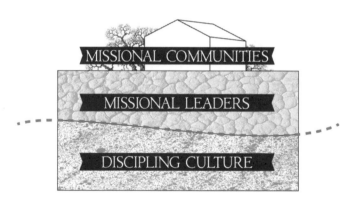

We need to count the cost as leaders, because this takes tenacity and prayer and perseverance. But the good news is that God is with us in this. It's His Kingdom we're seeking to advance, He told us to make disciples, and He will empower us to do so. These are God's dreams for our cities, and He will lead us and guide us as we seek Him. So keep your eyes on the prize. Imagine what it will look like when you've been able to build a discipling culture and release your leaders effectively into mission beyond the church walls. Keep this in mind as you seek to move your church into a more missional lifestyle through building a discipling culture.

APPENDIX 2

∿ YOU GO FIRST: ∿ STARTING A PILOT MC

CHANGE YOUR LIFE, CHANGE THE WORLD

Because we place such high value on **leaders going first** and offering their lives as examples for others to imitate, we coach pastors to actually lead an MC themselves before trying to launch them in their church. It doesn't matter if you pastor a mega-church, a medium-sized church, or a church plant. It's not enough to explain the theory of MCs to people who have never actually experienced it. They need to experience and understand it before they go and lead one. You can't coach people in something you've never actually done. You can't lead people to a place you've never gone.

The first thing is to simply begin to apply the principles listed at the beginning of this book to your own life! Begin to live as a family on mission, and invite people to join you. If you as the pastor are not beginning to live differently, MCs will simply function as another program, and never take off as the seedbed for *oikos*.

In addition to beginning to live this stuff out, we also coach pastors to help equip their leaders to do what they have begun to do by launching what we call a *Pilot Missional Community*. It's rooted in all the same principles we've discussed in this book, of course, but a couple of nuances are worth noting. Here's a rough outline of what that could look like.

WHAT IS A PILOT MISSIONAL COMMUNITY?

A Pilot MC is a collection of 20–40 Christian leaders who are learning to lead a future MC by participating in the Pilot. Like all MCs, they will regularly do UP (deepening their relationship with God), IN (deepening their relationship with each other), and OUT (deepening their relationships with people who don't know Jesus yet).

What is the purpose and outcome of the Pilot Missional Community?

The purpose of the Pilot MC is to teach these future MC leaders how to lead an extended family on mission. They will be immersed in an experience that you will then challenge them to live out personally. The purpose is not necessarily to grow the group or do long-term mission. This group will exist for a temporary season of training, and then the leaders will be dispersed to lead various MCs. These expectations should be communicated clearly at the start of the Pilot MC so people are aware and have appropriate expectations. The desired outcome of the Pilot MC is as follows:

- **ONE:** Leaders experience of a group of 20–40 people doing UP, IN, and OUT. Most people are familiar with how to lead smaller-sized groups but are quite unfamiliar with this larger-sized group. You want them to walk away thinking, "Wow, I really like how a group that size feels and functions together."

- **TWO:** Leaders have a chance to lead a few MC experiences within the Pilot before they are released to lead their own. Rather than expecting someone to lead something they've never even tried leading, the Pilot allows leaders a safe environment to lead something new, where failure won't be a disaster.

- **THREE:** Leaders get to feel out the natural rhythms of UP, IN, and OUT over an extended period of time and how that pattern of life builds a center of gravity for the MC as they commit to the *organized* and the *organic* elements of their life together.

IS THERE A GOOD METAPHOR FOR UNDERSTANDING A PILOT MISSIONAL COMMUNITY THAT I CAN SHARE WITH OUR LEADERS TO HELP THEM UNDERSTAND IT?

Giving people a metaphor really helps them understand the purpose of what you're doing and what you're asking them to do. The metaphor we've used before is Boot Camp. We aren't in the heat of battle yet, but we are training for it. Currently, we've got a bunch of paintball guns, and when something explodes, it's just paint. But you're doing your best to create an environment that simulates what it's actually like and give them the training they need to succeed.

HOW LONG DOES A PILOT MISSIONAL COMMUNITY LAST?

We strongly recommend at least six to nine months, particularly if you are relatively new to leading an MC. We know some pastors want to do it for three to four months (because they can squeeze it into a Sept-Dec or Jan-April time slot), but ultimately, we think you're doing yourself a disservice by truncating it. If the desired outcomes are the three things mentioned above, we don't know how to do it in less than six to nine months. Of course, we're excited to send people out to the missional frontier, but we want leaders out there who have been adequately trained so they can succeed. Perhaps the only thing worse than never sending people out to lead is sending poorly trained, ill-equipped people out to lead. People who get sent out poorly equipped to lead usually never try it again.

Don't let excitement lead to impatience. The short-term pain for you as a leader of patiently investing pays off immensely in the medium- and long-term fruit of well-trained and fruitful leaders. Remember, it takes a while to train a leader, so don't fall into the mentality of plugging volunteers into a program. Your leaders will be the collateral damage in this scenario, and then you probably won't get a second chance. Plan to go at least six to nine months.

HOW MANY TIMES A MONTH DOES THE PILOT MISSIONAL COMMUNITY NEED TO MEET?

The nitty-gritty answer is you'll need three to four scheduled (organized) times a month. If you remember the organized–organic continuum, you'll realize that there will be other times you choose to get the group together for an organic, more spontaneous activity. That's normal for families, right? So, while you have some things scheduled, there might be movies, baseball games, girls' nights, guys' nights, barbecues, etc. This may mean, however, that people might need to shift their schedule a little or pull back from some church activities during this time. As the leader, you'll need to help them navigate this.

The bottom line is that if you don't spend enough time together as an MC doing UP, IN, and OUT, people won't really experience the texture of MC life adequately. It really doesn't work as an "add-on" to someone's life.

HOW DO HUDDLES PLAY INTO THE PILOT MISSIONAL COMMUNITY?

ONE: Huddle is a discipling vehicle for leaders that involves training, discipleship, support, and accountability. Pick up a copy of *Building a Discipling Culture*, which is all about Huddles and discipling leaders. You'll need to do Huddle well if your Pilot MC is going to produce the results you want to see.

TWO: The people in your Pilot MC will need to learn how to disciple leaders through the vehicle of Huddle. That means they will need to be in a short-term Huddle within your Pilot MC. In many ways, it will feel like a Pilot Huddle.

THREE: We've seen this happen best when the person leading the Pilot MC has already been Huddling a group of six to eight people before the Pilot MC starts. Then, the people you've been Huddling will lead the small groups/ Huddles that happen in the Pilot MC.

FOUR: Don't add an extra night for Huddle. Huddle the people in the Pilot MC twice a month, but fold it into a time when everyone is already together. See more details on this a little further down.

FIVE: When the Pilot MC comes to a close and new MCs are launched, make sure you continue to Huddle those new MC leaders. They will need you even more when they start their own MCs!

WHAT'S THE PURPOSE OF THE OUT WEEKS IF WE'RE NOT TRYING TO GROW THE GROUP?

The best way to use OUT weeks is to do various OUT activities together. The purpose of these times is not to commit to one specific mission for your six to nine months together, but to give your future MC leaders a taste of lots of different ways to do OUT. You have the opportunity to expand their missional imagination. Chances are, you will have kids in your Pilot MC, so you'll need to think through that with your OUT weeks as well. Use some of them to do family-friendly OUTs and others to do adult-only OUTs. See the end of this section for a list of OUT suggestions for a Pilot MC.

SAMPLE MONTHLY RHYTHM

There are many ways to structure your monthly rhythm in a Pilot MC. Please don't see this as a formula or a prescription in any way. This is simply a rhythm we have found helpful. After giving the rhythm, we'll explain a little further about it.

Week 1: UP

Week 2: IN - Thanksgiving meal + Small Groups.

Week 3: OUT

Week 4: IN - Thanksgiving meal + Small Groups.

UP WEEK EXAMPLE

6:30   Give an overview of the night, opening prayer.

6:35   Read the Scripture for the night and sing two to four worship songs.

6:55   Have six to eight people read a passage of Scripture that's impacted them in the last two weeks and talk about what God has been saying to them from it, or have them share a story of breakthrough.

7:15   MC leader reads the Scripture for the night again and gives a five- to eight-minute meditation on it.

7:25   Break up into small groups of six to eight. Each group is led by a trained leader (people in your Huddle). Help people answer, "What is God saying right now?" Then have people share prayer requests and engage in a time of prayer with each other.

7:50   Groups come back together. If any "big" prayer requests come out of small group time, the whole group spends time in prayer.

8:00   MC leader gives closing thought. Sing one last song. Blessing.

8:10   Dismiss

IN WEEK EXAMPLE

6:00   Everyone brings enough food for their family + 2 to share and eat together.

6:15   Every person, one by one, shares something he or she is thankful for. Pray.

6:30   Eat together.

7:15   Break into small groups of four to eight people, each led by a trained leader (groups have the same leader for whole Pilot MC).

8:25   Groups come back together. If any "big" prayer requests come out of Huddle time, the whole group spends time in prayer.

8:30   Dismiss

OUT WEEK EXAMPLE

Here are several suggestions for OUT weeks. Notice these are really low-bar suggestions that aren't intimidating or difficult. There are a million things you could do for these weeks, and you'll probably have some great ideas based on your context and experience. These are simply a few we have found that work well. We hope the examples stir your imagination—don't put OUT in a box!

Before each time OUT, spend a few minutes praying asking that God's Kingdom will come, that the relationships of the MC will really show the life of Jesus to others.

FAMILY-FRIENDLY OUT SUGGESTIONS

*   Have a kickball or soccer game in the park on a Saturday and invite your friends and their kids.

*   Get a video projector and some speakers and project a family movie on the back of your house (or inside on a wall if it's raining!). Have everyone invite their friends.

*   Take a prayer walk around the neighborhood with the kids. Note the earlier instructions for how to do a prayer walk (page 107).

- Go to a family-friendly restaurant or event and intentionally talk to people there who aren't part of your Pilot MC.

- Have the whole Pilot MC go to one of the kids' soccer or tee-ball games and get to know the other parents in the stands.

ADULT-FRIENDLY OUT SUGGESTIONS

- Throw a party and invite your People of Peace friends. Easy!

- Find people in your neighborhood who could use some help around the house and invite People of Peace to help you bless your neighbors.

- Have the people in the MC divide into groups of several families each, plan a dinner, invite People of Peace to the dinner, and just hang out.

- Have the whole group run a 5K together to raise money for a local charity through per-mile donations. Invite People of Peace to join you in fundraising, running, and partying afterward!

Of course, these are just guidelines and suggestions—there are many different ways a Pilot MC can play out. A large established church even used a Pilot MC to start an entirely new church plant in the downtown area of their city. Here's their story:

> "A small community of leaders had been dreaming of living out the mission of Jesus in the downtown area of our city for several years. In March 2013, we started a Pilot Missional Community that met in a homeless day center in the heart of downtown.
>
> After a couple of months establishing rhythms, building relationships with People of Peace, and serving various needs in the city, we felt called to center our mission on an urban park near the campus of a major university downtown. The neighborhood around the park is socially and economically diverse, with rich and poor, college students, a large population of skaters, as well as many homeless.
>
> Moving into the summer, we moved our MC gatherings into the neighborhood around the park at a local church, as well as throwing a party in the park every other Sunday night in order to meet and engage our neighbors in the city. So far, this has done wonders to help us engage people outside our MC with free food and conversation, as well as provide a non-religious environment to

invite our People of Peace.

Our vision for the fall of 2013 is to multiply into two to three MCs in the downtown area, while starting our first weekend service toward the beginning of 2014. We're excited to see what God has in store for our family on mission in the months ahead, as we seek to be good news to our city's downtown area!"[34]

---

[34] See "Appendix 4: MCs and Church Planting" on page 133 for principles on church planting using MCs.

APPENDIX 3

∾ WHAT ABOUT OUR ∾
CURRENT PROGRAMS?

Chances are you already have some kind of small-group structure active in your church. What should you do with these groups if you want to transition your church to using MCs?

The first thing is that it's a bad idea to simply kill all the small groups and announce from the pulpit that everyone will now be doing MCs. Don't do that. Instead, simply begin to talk about, in sermons and conversations, what it looks like to live life like Jesus: UPward toward God, INward toward one another in the Body of Christ, and OUTward toward those around us who don't know Jesus. Tell people you are starting to look at this and want to implement it in your own life, and begin to talk about a vision of communities that act like extended families with Kingdom mission that live UP, IN, and OUT together.

Then see what happens as God begins to speak to people. Notice who responds and wants to know more. Observe who shows energy and interest in perhaps being part of one of these "UP/IN/OUT" groups. They are probably the people to begin casting more specific vision for MCs to. Not everyone will respond, and that's OK.

Generally speaking, we have found that small groups tend to go in one of four directions in response to this vision for mission:

STAY

Some small groups don't do anything. They just stay a small group like before, not really responding to the vision.

JOIN

Sometimes, several small groups join together to form a new MC because they find they have a shared missional vision.

MULTIPLY

Sometimes if a small group discovers that its members have different missional visions, the group moves into two or three new small groups that can function as the seeds of new MCs.

GROW

Finally, if the leader of a small group has the vision and capacity to lead an MC, sometimes a small group grows into an MC (which then has small groups within it) as they gather people around the missional vision.

Any of these responses is OK! If folks don't catch the vision initially and simply want to remain as a small group, leave them be, and invest your energy in those who want to step into mission. This is really important—don't invest your energy trying to get everyone to the starting line at the same time. This is more like a staggered start, with you investing in the early adopters first, who then become models for those who respond later. The stayers may come around later, but it's not worth it to try and kill a group or force it to change.

The temptation is to believe there is a model or formula for all of this. There isn't. Every church context is different, and as a pastor, you have the privilege of discerning, with your leadership team, what God is doing in your context.

HUDDLES, MISSIONAL COMMUNITIES, AND SMALL GROUPS, OH MY!

Sometimes people have more questions about Huddles, MCs, and small groups, such as the following:

- What's the difference between a Huddle and a small group?
- Are we suggesting that Huddles replace small groups?

First let's talk about the differences. The easiest way to highlight this is by describing exactly what a Huddle is.

A Huddle is a place for leaders to receive investment, training, an example to imitate, and accountability—in other words: discipleship! The most important thing to note about Huddle: **It is for current and/or future leaders.** The people accepting an invitation into a Huddle should know that they are expected to eventually lead something (if they aren't already). This is the principle at work: If you disciple leaders in how to disciple people, everyone in your community will be discipled. Why? Because you're instilling in your leaders the Great Commission principle that every disciple disciples others. It's making disciples who make disciples.

A Huddle is by invitation only. A Huddle is an invitation for six to 12 leaders to regularly receive intentional investment from a discipling leader. But it is more than that. It's also an invitation in that leader's life, not just for a 90-minute gathering once a week. You have access to the life of the discipling leader outside the official Huddle time. As the people in the Huddle interact with the Huddle leader in structured and spontaneous environments, discipleship ends up taking deeper root because it is *caught* as well as *taught*.

A Huddle is something that is reproduced. Rather than adding people to a Huddle, we multiply the discipling culture because every person in the Huddle will be infusing the discipleship DNA into whatever they lead. For example, rather than "growing" a Huddle from eight people to 12 people, we equip and train the eight people to lead something that is infused with the discipleship DNA. Now instead of one group with eight people, we have nine groups with perhaps 50 people (the original group of eight, plus eight groups of perhaps six each). It's about investing in multiplication leading to exponential growth instead of addition leading to linear growth.

A Huddle is a place for invitation and challenge. Huddle leaders, as they invest in the lives of the people in their Huddles, invite them into their life and their rhythms and have access to their spiritual capital. However, Huddle leaders also bring challenge (gracefully) to those in the Huddle to live more fully in the Kingdom when their way of life is different or out of step with the Kingdom.

A Huddle is high commitment. For all the reasons stated above.
In contrast to Huddles, here are some generalizations about the way most churches use small groups (note that every church does these things a bit differently):

- Small groups are usually much less commitment.

- Anyone can be part of a small group. It is an open community.

- Challenge is not as regular an element in most small groups, because the emphasis is typically on creating a welcoming environment for newcomers.

- Small groups are usually led by facilitators who are looking to create space for everyone to share and contribute.

- Small groups grow by adding members, and multiply when they become too big. It's growth by addition.

- Small groups tend to lean toward the lowest common denominator in terms of spiritual content so that anyone can step in.

DON'T KILL YOUR small groups and try to replace them with Huddles.

If you're trying to implement MCs and Huddles, and you've already got small groups, you're probably still going to need small groups. As we've said, don't kill your small groups and try to replace them with Huddles. Instead, understand the difference between the two and distinguish them in your spiritual formation process. The best way to transition is to look for new leaders to start new MCs and then, as they grow, implement small groups in these new MCs. In addition, identify the small group leaders who seem to have the vision and capacity to lead an MC and work with them to grow their small group into an MC. Note that the majority of small groups will stay small groups initially.

Huddles focus on leaders and future leaders. If you Huddle leaders and disciple them, invest in them, give them an easily transferrable and portable discipling language, teach them how to disciple others, and teach them how to calibrate invitation and challenge in discipling individuals and groups, then they'll be able to do this in all kinds of spiritual formation vehicles (small groups, triads, one-on-one mentoring, Sunday school, etc.). The essential question is, Do you have a leader who has been trained to disciple people, and can he or she import that into any setting? That's what investing in a leader through Huddle does.

A well-trained discipling leader makes any vehicle more effective in discipling people, including small groups. Training leaders in Huddle is the way the

DNA of the discipling culture spreads throughout the entire organism of your church. But you don't actually need everyone in a Huddle to get there. You just need your leaders and future leaders in Huddles.

Here's a helpful diagram we often use to explain this visually. For churches that have vehicles at each of these three sociological spaces (public space = worship service, social space = MCs, personal space = small groups), it can often look like this:

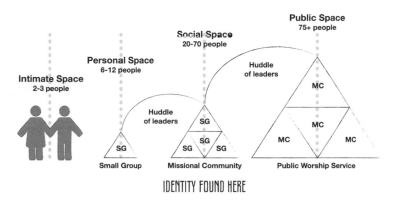

IDENTITY FOUND HERE

The Huddles act like the ligaments and tendons that hold the "bones" of the body together, allowing it to stay connected, coordinated, and flexible!

A WORD ON ORBITS AND TENSIONS

We have said that MCs orbit a central church. This means that MCs are not a *substitute* for Sunday services altogether. It is important to come together as the wider people of God for celebration and worship. However, as MCs gain traction in mission, they often begin to meet more often in their mission context. When this happens, they usually begin to orbit the central church by gathering with the whole church on some Sundays and gathering in their mission context on other Sundays (at a school hall, a park, someone's house, etc.).

As a rule of thumb, we have found that most mature MCs gather with the wider church at a service no less than once a month and no more than three times a month.

Clearly, this is possible only if we are creating a low-control, high-accountability culture. **Low control** means that MCs are not told how they should operate or what they should do. It is the responsibility of the MC leader to determine the rhythm of his or her community, based on the vision, context, and season. **High accountability** means that in whatever rhythm MCs adopt, we are holding them accountable for being healthy and missionally purposeful. We want MCs to be missionally effective in their context, but we also want to help them foster a connection to the wider church. In this way, we encourage a regular diet of accountability, mission, community, public worship, and teaching.

The central church then becomes a place of training, equipping, prayer, resourcing, and encouragement for each MC. Each MC has a defined orbit around the central church; this means that some communities may come to Sunday gatherings most weeks and meet out in the community one Sunday a month (and on weekdays at other times), or they might meet most weeks out in their community context and come back to the center just once a month. Or it could be anything in between!

This involves a normal and healthy tension that needs to be navigated. You will want to equip and release your MCs to be incarnationally present in their mission contexts, but you still need people to work in the nursery on Sunday mornings. As a pastor, you need to be willing to work through these tensions and talk openly and honestly with your leaders about it.

Truly releasing your MC leaders will require a re-allocation of time, energy, and money that will involve stretching and growing into a new way of operating. **It is far more comfortable to do "just organic church" (MC only) or "just big church" (church service only). But you can release tremendous missional potential if you embrace the tension and attend to both, because they feed off and influence each other in extremely catalytic ways.**

> **TRULY RELEASING** your MC leaders will require a re-allocation of time, energy, and money that will involve stretching and growing into a new way of operating.

We fully understand that this will sound quite radical to some. It's not an easy thing for a church to do, because it can feel like we are undervaluing what has gone before. However, as the cultural context of the Western world continues to change dramatically, we believe that we need to rethink what it means to be the church, that we cannot afford to simply try to prop up the structures of the past simply because it is uncomfortable to reshape them. Our deep conviction is that it is worth it. Embrace the tension of committing yourself to *oikos* and the centralized resource center that church can become.

APPENDIX 4
~ MCs AND ~ CHURCH PLANTING

IS THIS CHURCH PLANTING?

Pastors often ask us how leading MCs relates to church planting. Although there are certainly some similarities (we've said that MCs are kind of like "little churches"), there are some key differences between an MC and a church plant.

Unlike church plants, MCs remain integrally involved with the sending church. Most of the time, church plants function as autonomous entities, with their own leadership and systems that are independent from the mother church. MCs, on the other hand, are not independent, autonomous congregations. They continue to rely on the resources provided by the central church for their ongoing support, accountability, training, and equipping, and thus continue to belong to the overall family of the central church.

Unlike church plants, the *overall* vision for the MCs is set by the sending church. With a church plant, an entirely new vision is often what brings about the church plant. The vision of an MC, however, functions as "a vision within the vision," a specific outworking of the overall vision in a particular neighborhood or relational network.

Unlike church plants, MCs are highly mobile and flexible, able to move from the places they meet at a moment's notice. A church plant typically needs a consistent place to meet in order to establish continuity and presence in a community. An MC, because it exists as part of a wider worshiping body, can afford to be far more flexible in meeting times and locations.

Unlike church plants, the leaders of MCs are not paid. This is part of what makes them such a great lightweight/low-maintenance vehicle for mission and discipleship. Although a church plant typically involves highly trained specialist staff who are paid full- or part-time for the work they do, MCs are always led by volunteers.

Unlike church plants, MCs are not financially independent; they give their tithes to the sending church for them to redistribute as appropriate. As discussed before, MCs do not collect tithes or have bank accounts, but remain financially connected to the central church. Offerings (above and beyond tithes) can of course be taken in an MC for needs or projects that arise, but an MC does not operate as a church or nonprofit, collecting general donations.

Unlike church plants, MCs are called to reproduce new MCs. One could argue that church plants ought to produce new church plants, of course, and we know many churches that are committed to this. But multiplication is built into every MC's DNA from the very beginning, which sets them apart from a typical church plant.

Unlike church plants, MCs do not necessarily meet every Sunday in a central church building. Typically in church planting, those who are going to be part of the new church meet every Sunday with the new community to establish it. Even the most pioneering MC, however, continues to orbit a central church by attending a worship gathering at least once a month.

> **MCs ARE A VEHICLE** that helps us re-form *oikos* (extended families on mission together), which is a pretty good description of what the New Testament calls church.

Unlike church plants, MCs are resourced primarily by the sending church, not by themselves. An MC continues to orbit a central church, as we mentioned above. This means that the central church remains the source from which the MC receives support and training, as opposed to a church plant, where these resources would be developed from within.

Those things being said, MCs are a vehicle that helps us re-form *oikos* (extended families on mission together), which is a pretty good description of what the New Testament calls church. So you could think of launching MCs as lightweight/low-maintenance church planting if you want! Many people we know have used MCs as a framework for developing a church planting strategy, multiplying MCs to become the core team of a new church plant. The next section features some notes on this process from people who have done this.

PLANTING A CHURCH USING MISSIONAL COMMUNITIES

As the Western world becomes increasingly "post-Christian," our church-planting strategies need to adapt to this new reality. Of course, there is no one right way to plant a church when considering MCs, but as people who have planted with MCs and coached hundreds of church planters using MCs as a vehicle, we would like to share a few of the things we've learned along the way.

Obviously, you need to contextualize this information to your city, your culture, your team, your gifts, and your calling. Many times, the temptation for church planters is to look for a "pure model" and rigidly stick to that formula no matter what (this can have disastrous results). We've found there's no such thing as a pure way to plant a church. You need to contextualize Jesus' principles for discipleship and mission for your context, which will undoubtedly look at least a little different in each church plant.

That said, we think that the **DNA of multiplication** can be a helpful place to start.

The key to success for any church hoping to use MCs is building the DNA of multiplication Into the church from the start. We want to see multiplication on every level: multiplying disciples, vehicles for discipleship and mission, campuses, and even churches. Multiplication results in exponential growth, while addition results in only linear growth.

THE KEY TO SUCCESS
for any church hoping to use MCs is building the DNA of multiplication into the church from the start.

You've probably heard most of the illustrations about the power of exponential growth vs. linear growth. For example, if you were able to keep folding a piece of paper in half indefinitely (essentially doubling its height every fold), it would take you only 42 folds to *reach the moon*. Or, if you started with one dollar and doubled your money every day, by the end of the first week you'd have $64. But **by the end of the first month, you'd have $268,435,456!**

This is the kind of process we want to put into the DNA of our church plant from the very beginning, but it's easier said than done. *It is always easier to grow by addition than by multiplication.* It will always be easier to simply attract more people to a meeting than it is to train someone to multiply what you're doing, because the results are quicker and more easily quantifiable. But if you choose addition, you limit your rate of growth in the long run. Multiplication is what we're after, and while it's a difficult thing to learn with MCs on the front end when planting a church, it's worth it in the end when you hit the tipping point of the exponential process.

The first year of church planting is usually the most important as you are setting the cultural DNA of your community, dealing with wet cement, and things will soon solidify. If your cultural DNA concretizes without the element of multiplication, it's a much harder task to put it in later.

What does this mean practically?

Start with the thing you want to multiply (one MC) instead of starting something different (a "church service") and trying to launch MCs later. The worship service will come later, but when you are gathering your core team, cast vision for and recruit them into being a family on mission. In essence, start an MC. This will help you to have the right DNA from the outset.

If you can multiply MCs, the worship service will be easy, because chances are you already know how to lead that vehicle really well, and the worship service will actually end up feeling like an overflow of the life people are experiencing in MCs instead of the one vehicle we're trying to use to create it.

Give your core team a metaphor

To be clear, we are suggesting you *wait to start a worship service until you feel confident in your community's ability to multiply disciples and MCs.* But that will take some time, and because almost everyone equates church with "worship service," it will be crucial to the development of your core team for you to give them a metaphor to understand what they are doing. Remember that it will look quite different from what they normally think of as church, and will take more time. If people don't understand *why* you're using this approach, they will quickly become frustrated and disenchanted.

Giving people a metaphor (and then making sure you talk about that metaphor over and over) helps them understand the purpose of what you're doing and what you're asking them to do. It gives them handles to understand the new thing you're calling them into.

There are many metaphors you can use. At the end of the day, you may want to use one that is completely original. But allow us to give you a couple of examples we've used before:

1. **Boot Camp**

    In this first MC, you aren't in the heat of spiritual battle yet, but you are training for it. Right now, you've got a bunch of paintball guns, and when something explodes, it's just paint. But you're doing your best to create an environment that simulates what it's actually like and giving them the training they need to succeed.

    With this first Missional Community, you are exploring together what it feels like to operate as an extended family on mission (*oikos*). You are using this experience to train people how to disciple people and lead out in mission with a family, incarnating and proclaiming the gospel of Jesus wherever you go. (Remember that you will probably need a minimum of 12–15 adults in your core team so it immediately functions like an extended family.)

2. **Motorcycle Gang (not Charter Bus)**

    An MC is really just an extended family on mission where everyone is able to participate out of their Holy Spirit gifting for the building up of everyone else, allowing people to become spiritual initiators who don't just come to church and *hear* the Word (and so deceive themselves) but those also who *do* the Word, those who really put Jesus' teachings into practice in community and mission.

    So instead of being like a charter bus, where one or two people do most of the work and everyone else sits and enjoys the ride, planting with MCs is more like a being a **motorcycle gang**: Almost everyone has something to do. We might be driving different kinds of motorcycles for different reasons, and perhaps driving on different parts of the road, **but we're a gang**: We stick together and support one another, and we have a *culture* together that keeps us all moving in the same direction together.

Whatever metaphor you choose, we've found it's very important to keep talking about it and reminding people every time you gather why you are doing what you're doing.

As you live UP, IN, and OUT in this first MC, you will be discipling people, and eventually you will have several leaders emerge from who are ready to start MCs of their own.

And now you've started to multiply.

Start a worship service when you have at least 75+ adults

Resist the urge to start a worship service until you have *at least* 75 adults (and probably more like 80–90). This means you will have multiplied your original MC and probably have at least three MCs (though this is not a hard-and-fast rule). Again, the temptation will always be to start it sooner, but if you don't have the mass needed to make it a true "public space" gathering, the social dynamics of a smaller group of people will quickly feel insular and stale.

RESIST THE URGE to start a worship service until you have at least 75 adults

Before you start a weekly worship service, you may want to start doing a worship service once a month for your core team once you've multiplied into two MCs. You'll want to do this in a space that's appropriate for the size of your group. If you have 50 adults, you'll want a room that feels appropriate for that size group.

This will give your core team hope that you are moving toward a worship service (which is an important part of a church expression) as well as giving you a chance to explore what it looks like to lead a worship service in a way that is true to your cultural DNA. It also allows you to learn how to make a worship service lightweight and low maintenance.

Different models for starting a worship service

Here are a few different ways to start your worship service. Again, there is no right way, and each model has strengths and weaknesses.

- **Centralized approach.** Start once a month, ramp up slowly, and eventually get to meeting every week. This will put more on people's calendars, but if you've discipled them well in how to order and balance their life, this can work really well.

- **Decentralized approach.** Start meeting for your worship services more frequently and then slowly back off to meeting corporately once a month. This makes MCs the dominant expression of your church community and makes the worship service an overflow/celebration event.

- **Lean into the tension**. Start meeting weekly in the worship service right off the bat (after getting 80–90 adults in MCs), knowing it will be a season of needing to put energy into the worship service, shifting some of your community's focus from the "Home" dynamic and leaning into the "Temple" dynamic.[35] Prepare leaders for this, but also make sure you eventually lean back into "Home" at some point; otherwise, people will get the impression all that MC stuff was for before when we didn't have this church service!

Again, there is no one-size-fits-all answer. You will need wisdom from the Holy Spirit on which model (or hybrid thereof) is right for your community. Each presents challenges and opportunities that you will need to attend to.

Here is our biggest caveat: Left to their own devices, most church planters will plant a church that is in *reaction* to a model they've experienced and disliked. Either you thought there was too much emphasis on the worship service or too little, too much emphasis on being decentralized or too little. Or you felt the worship service wasn't done to your liking, or their discipleship process didn't work like yours will. It's easy to engage in ditch-to-ditch thinking, jumping from one ditch to the other and (to mix our metaphors) throwing the baby out with the bathwater.

Choose to live in tension

What we need to learn to do is live in the tension of embracing the Temple

---

[35] This is actually a very important dynamic to understand. See Chapter 9 of our book *Leading Kingdom Movements* for more information.

experience (the worship service) and the Home experience (Missional Communities), learning to lean into one or the other based on how God is leading you and what is needed at the time.

If you're doing this well, you will never escape the need to navigate the tensions of time and energy once you start a centralized gathering. The worship service will inevitably pull time and energy away from MCs and the organic life happening there. However, we argue that the healthy organic life of MCs cannot be sustained for the long haul apart from the regular celebration service.

What we need to learn to do is establish a "low center of gravity," so we can keep our balance, spreading our weight across the continuum of Temple and Home. When we do this, we can respond to situations and the Spirit's leading appropriately, leaning one way or the other without losing our balance. Maturity means that we are able to lean into Temple without abandoning Home, and vice versa. We need to learn what is necessary and sufficient for each, knowing how to do a "full-fledged" and "bare-bones" version of each.

Find an economic engine

The thing about planting a church this way is that it's slower than other methods, so the metrics are different. Let us be clear on what we mean by that: *You won't have a full-time salary in two years.* We would recommend against using only church/denominational support and personal fundraising as your only economic engine. The pressure of needing to "come up with a salary" will skew things in a wonky direction, and you will unwittingly make decisions about the future of the church that have more to do with money than what God has called your community to.

So if you're exploring the option of being bivocational (which we recommend), here are some key criteria to think through when it comes to your tent-making profession.

1. It should be flexible, allowing it coexist nicely with planting a church and having a family.
2. It should pay the bills with a little to spare.
3. It should not be too emotionally taxing. Church planting is hard enough on the emotions. (In other words, commission-based sales might be a bad idea!)

4. If possible, it should overlap well with missional opportunities you can involve the church in (again, this is flexible/optional, but it's icing on the cake if you can get it).

To apply these ideas, let's consider two of the more popular bivocational jobs for church planters: barista and web designer.

BARISTA

1. **Flexible? Yes!** You can work early morning hours, afternoon, or night, depending on what works best for your missional context.

2. **Pays the bills with room to spare? Nope!** Even with a place like Starbucks covering some health insurance, it's just over minimum wage, which isn't sustainable for a family.

3. **Not emotionally taxing? Yes!** You can clock in and clock out, and the job requires little of your emotional or cognitive faculties.

4. **Blends into missional space? Yes!** Being a barista is a great way to meet a lot of new people, many of whom will likely be People of Peace.

FREELANCE WEB DESIGNER

1. **Flexible? Yes!** Besides meetings with clients, you basically work whenever you want.

2. **Pays the bills with room to spare? Sort of.** Most web-designing church planters we know combine this with support-raising and the church paying some of their salary.

3. **Not emotionally taxing? Sort of.** Most web designers we know find the work emotionally invigorating, functioning as a creative outlet. The problem with freelancing is that you can't just be a great designer. You also have to be constantly seeking out new business and selling your services to new clients.

4. **Blends into missional space? Yes!**

Both jobs probably aren't good options as your only source of income, but could work decently when combined with other things. In fact, we recommend seeking out multiple sources of income anyway. Even though it's a bit messier than just having one job, it's more robust and sustainable long-term, because you don't have all your eggs in one basket.

What we encourage church planters to do is be brutally honest about how long it's going to take to plant the church, about what funds will be necessary to plant, and about bivocational options. This may mean that you need to spend an additional year or two learning a new skill before planting that you can use while planting.

LEARNING COMMUNITIES

As we mentioned above, a book can only take you so far, which is why we've developed the Learning Community process to help leaders and strategic teams navigate these transitions successfully. We have seen hundreds of churches come through this process, and while the personal and cultural challenges are significant, through the process of being coached and trained in navigating the transition we have seen churches all over the Western world begin to see significant fruit in the areas of discipleship and mission.

The process is almost always messy and slow, personally challenging, and painful in some ways. But through God's grace, it is *doable*. We pray that will encourage you to lean into the dreams God has put in your heart for Kingdom breakthrough in your city.

You can find out more about Learning Communities and other resources on our website: *www.weare3dm.com*.